ZERO
HOUR
AMERICA

HISTORY'S ULTIMATUM
OVER FREEDOM AND THE
ANSWER WE MUST GIVE

OS GUINNESS

An imprint of InterVarsity Press
Downers Grove, Illinois

InterVarsity Press
P.O. Box 1400 | Downers Grove, IL 60515-1426
ivpress.com | email@ivpress.com

InterVarsity Press® is the publishing division of InterVarsity Christian Fellowship/USA®. For more information, visit intervarsity.org.

All Scripture quotations, unless otherwise indicated, are taken from the New American Standard Bible®, copyright 1960, 1962, 1963, 1968, 1971, 1972, 1973, 1975, 1977, 1995 by The Lockman Foundation. Used by permission.

While any stories in this book are true, some names and identifying information may have been changed to protect the privacy of individuals.

Published in association with the literary agency of Wolgemuth & Associates.

The publisher cannot verify the accuracy or functionality of website URLs used in this book beyond the date of publication.

Cover design and image composite: David Fassett
Interior design: Jeanna Wiggins

ISBN 978-1-5140-0589-7 (print) | ISBN 978-1-5140-0591-0 (digital)

Printed in the United States of America ♾

Library of Congress Cataloging-in-Publication Data
Names: Guinness, Os, author.
Title: Zero hour America : history's ultimatum over freedom and the answer
  we must give / Os Guinness.
Description: Downers Grove, IL : IVP, InterVarsity Press, [2022] | Includes
  index.
Identifiers: LCCN 2022019794 (print) | LCCN 2022019795 (ebook) | ISBN
  9781514005897 (print) | ISBN 9781514005910 (digital)
Subjects: LCSH: Christianity and politics–United States–History–21st
  century. | Liberty–Religious aspects–Christianity–History–21st
  century. | Christianity and culture–United States–History–21st
  century. | United States–Moral conditions–21st century.
Classification: LCC BR516 .G855 2022 (print) | LCC BR516 (ebook) | DDC
  261.70973–dc23/eng/20220603
LC record available at https://lccn.loc.gov/2022019794
LC ebook record available at https://lccn.loc.gov/2022019795

29 28 27 26 25 24 23 22 | 9 8 7 6 5 4 3 2 1

DOM

And to John Brandon, Troy Griepp,

Dick Ohman, and Ryon Paton,

Four friends, one faith, undying gratitude.

The accurate knowledge of what has happened will be useful because according to human probability similar things will happen again.

THUCYDIDES, *HISTORY OF THE PELOPONNESIAN WAR*

The knowledge gained from the study of true history is the best of all educations for practical life. For it is history and history alone which, without involving us in actual danger, will mature our judgment and prepare us to take right views, whatever may be the crisis or posture of affairs.

POLYBIUS, *THE HISTORIES*

To be ignorant of what happened before you were born is to be a child forever.

MARCUS TULLIUS CICERO, *LETTERS TO BRUTUS*

What experience and history teaches us is this—that people and governments have never learned anything from history, or acted upon any lessons they might have drawn from it.

GEORG W. F. HEGEL, *LECTURES ON THE PHILOSOPHY OF HISTORY*

God of our father, known of old,
Lord of our far-flung battle line,
Beneath whose awful hand we hold
Dominion over palm and pine—
Lord God of hosts, be with us yet,
Lest we forget, lest we forget....

Far-called, our navies melt away;
On dune and headland sinks the fire:
Lo, all our pomp of yesterday
Is one with Nineveh and Tyre!
Judge of the Nations, spare us yet,
Lest we forget—lest we forget!

RUDYARD KIPLING, "RECESSIONAL" 1897

Alexander the Great remarked that the people of Asia were slaves because they had not learned to pronounce the word "No." Let that not be the epitaph of the English speaking peoples.

WINSTON S. CHURCHILL, "THE DEFENCE OF FREEDOM"

Of the twenty-two civilizations that have appeared in history, nineteen of them collapsed when they reached the moral state the United States is in now.

ARNOLD TOYNBEE, *A STUDY OF HISTORY*

CONTENTS

PART ONE: THE URGENCY OF THE HOUR

  1 America Will Fall—Unless   3

  2 Under Our Own Vine and Fig Tree   13

  3 No Political Masterpiece?   19

  4 The Completest Revolution of All?   29

  5 An Offset for the Reset?   46

PART TWO: FREEDOM'S FOUNDATION STONES

  6 Set Free to Be Free   61

  7 Understood Upward   88

  8 The Essentials of Life   100

  9 Ordering Freedom   107

  10 Freedom, the Greatest Enemy of Freedom   120

  11 Righting Wrongs   127

  12 Passing the Baton   146

PART THREE: ULTIMATUM

  13 Zero Hour America   165

Index   195

PART ONE

THE URGENCY
OF THE HOUR

AMERICA WILL FALL—UNLESS

HOWL, AMERICA! HOWL! Howl like the Hebrew prophets howled over the fate of their people before the destruction of Jerusalem in 586 BC! Howl like Allen Ginsberg, the radical poet of the Beat generation, howled for the best minds of his generation, destroyed by madness in the 1950s! Howl for the way the fabled "land of the free" has turned its back on what made it free and is pursuing phantoms that lead to decline and ruin. Howl for how America has come to be what the world sees today—a world superpower still, wealthy, prosperous, and powerful but unrecognizable in terms of the ideals of its past and stumbling leaderless from one blunder to another. Howl for the way America is blindly ignoring its day of reckoning and opting for its own decline, careless about what it would take to avert it. Howl for the way a society fostering so much hate between its citizens appears to be yearning for its own destruction.

Have Americans forgotten their great *why*? The thousand and one ways their ancestors were not free elsewhere and the distinctive way that they were to live as a free people in the land of the free—with an ordered freedom born of freely chosen consent, a mutually binding pledge, and reciprocal responsibility of all for all? Not simply a democracy but a covenantal-constitutional republic that would witness to the world a better way of demonstrating human dignity, justice, freedom, and peace? Have Americans failed to realize that in choosing to be "one nation under God" they chose to be always accountable and always under the judgment of heaven for their deeds? Is America's stunning incomprehension about the present crisis the result of a blindness that is spiritual as well as intellectual?

America today makes no pretense of standing for the "great experiment" in freedom of its first president or the ordered freedom of the republic of its forebears and founders. America can no longer be called a shining city on a hill, an asylum for humanity, an almost chosen people, the last best hope of earth or an empire of liberty, let alone a people living "under God" and standing before the bar of history. Most Americans show little evidence that they understand freedom and the commitments that freedom requires of them. America now stands uncertainly, stunned and bemused through its ignorance of its enemies without and its enemies within. America's conscience is battered. America's public life is torn between the guilt of a sullied past, the pull of a power-hungry establishment oligarchy, and the countering pull of a radical left-wing revolution that has never worked anywhere or at any time, and that has always ended in failure and oppression. America after two and a half centuries has grown into a wealthy, elitist, technocratic, bureaucratic, and corporatist world power that alternately suppresses and squanders freedom with a prodigal carelessness that defies all reason—and despite all this still seems largely unaware of the deadliest peril it faces.

Is this how you Americans repay your ancestors, or is this heaven's judgment for all the sins and cynicism through which you have flouted or fallen short of your ideals over the years? Is this how you follow the intrepid men and women who braved the ocean in search of freedom? The patriots who staked their lives and fortunes on independence? The far-sighted band of leaders and thinkers who devised the ingenious ordering of constitutional freedom? The champions of justice and civil rights who addressed the monumental evils and hypocrisies of slavery that contradicted your ideals and hideously scarred your land? The generations who gave their lives for the freedom of others around the world and those they loved at home? The numberless unknown citizens who lived with dignity and decency and made it possible for you to live comfortably as Americans live today?

Is this how you enjoy the heritage of those who have gone before you? Is this the legacy you wish to hand to your children and their children's children? Is this the way you repay God in whom so many of your ancestors put their trust and from whom they received their ideals and their blessings? Shame on recent generations of Americans for their carelessness, their unconcern, and their ignorance of what the republic was founded to be. In contrast to those ideals, America today is enough to make every lover of freedom weep for the promise betrayed, the record stained indelibly, and the wide and gracious land crying out for the blood shed on it and the savageries committed in its name.

THE WRITING ON THE WALL

America will fall—unless. Like the writing on the wall at Belshazzar's feast, those four stern words will haunt America in a thousand variations unless the nation makes a wise and courageous decision to stop, think, and turn around, and then demonstrates that the consequences of the decision are real and lasting and not makeshift, cosmetic, or hypocritical. Recent events—from controversial elections to troubling responses to the global pandemic to the humanitarian and civic crisis on the southern border to domestic threats to free speech to the crippling national debt to the American humiliation and shame overseas to an intelligentsia directly at odds with the nation's beliefs to mounting questions about the character and stability of more than one president to the insane experiments in lifestyle pursued in the name of freedom, all together capping fifty years of drift and decline—must shake Americans awake, and a long-overdue debate about the real state of the union must begin. The American republic and its citizens now face titanic questions whose answers will prove decisive for the future of America.

First, is it wise and is it possible for Americans to switch revolutions in midcourse in history, and if not can they turn back? Having been founded on the ideals of ordered freedom in the American Revolution in 1776 (including, sadly, such blatant hypocrisy and contradiction as slavery), many Americans have recently shifted to the power-based legacies of the French Revolution in 1789—mediated through such movements as cultural Marxism, postmodernism, identity politics, the sexual revolution, and critical theory. With the current ignorance of history and the level of current conflicts and confusions, is it even possible for the present generation of Americans to remember their founding and restore its original promise? Or will America hasten its downfall through vacillating between the competing legacies of the two revolutions and harvesting the bitter fruits of uncertain and opposing views of freedom, justice, and political order?

Second, is it possible for America as the lead society of an immense civilization to examine its own conscience while at the height of its power, to make confession and amends for its evident wrongs—above all, for slavery and the treatment of the Native Americans—and to remedy, reform, and redirect its ways to the satisfaction of its citizens and the highest ideals of humanity? Or will America succumb to an orgy of politically organized recrimination and become the victim of its unforgiven past?

Third, will Americans recognize and respect the character of freedom and respond to freedom as freedom itself requires, or will they continue to follow faulty and specious views of freedom and remain satisfied with their distortions and imitations until they suffer irreversible decline? Not all who cry freedom have either the basis or the boundaries for the freedom they cry out for, and many of their views sound the death knell, not the Liberty Bell, for freedom, but can contemporary Americans tell the difference?

Fourth, in the momentous present crisis does America have the leaders with sufficient wisdom, courage, sense of history, and an understanding of the character of freedom to call Americans back, to guide the American people in considering and answering these questions and to do so in such a constructive way that they bring together a deeply divided people and reinvigorate a sense of united American identity and national purpose? Or will America slide leaderless toward decline?

These are watershed questions, and history and humanity wait for America's answer. But is America even facing up to such questions? Will America prove intellectually and morally capable of doing so? Americans must be in no doubt: neither freedom nor the faith that made freedom possible have let you down. You Americans have let down both faith and freedom, and it will be your tragedy if you blame the wrong sources, resort to false answers, and undermine faith and freedom with consequences that become irreversible. For one thing is certain and becoming clearer to more and more people by the day: *the radical left, the progressives, and the explosive arsenal of their protests and policies are as decisive a secession from the ideas and ideals of the American republic as the Southern states were from the Union in the Civil War.*

A CALL TO WAKE UP

"Let my people go!" "Let freedom ring!" "Let liberty be proclaimed throughout the land!" Nothing is more stirring to individual human beings than freedom. Freedom is one of God's greatest gifts to humanity. Human freedom is precious, human freedom is rare, human freedom is awesome in its mystery and its meaning. There is no other life form on planet earth with the capacity for freedom and responsibility that we humans have. Nothing is more essential and more fulfilling to our existence than freedom—the ability truly to be who we are, to think freely, to speak freely, and to choose and act freely in the fullest and most responsible possible way—and to be able to do so in community with others committed to living the same way. Nothing is more inspiring than working to liberate those who through no fault of their own are not free, and together with them and others, seeking to build and sustain societies that seek to fulfill the aspirations of freedom for every single one of their members.

This short book is no doomsday pronouncement. It is more of a Paul Revere's ride, though ironically the call to wake up this time is by a Brit and the warning is not about other enemies coming—the enemies are already within the gates. Even now when events in America are so often disheartening and at times angering, I remain confident that there are still Americans who will not give up on their great experiment in freedom, citizens for whom the cause of freedom remains unquenchable in their hearts, and leaders who know that the cause of freedom is moral, responsible, collective, and anything but selfish. Are there enough of such Americans? Are there leaders who will give them a voice? Who will be the ones to protect the torch of freedom in the present crisis? Are there still Americans who recognize that facing up to the challenge of America's decline is not an act of resignation but a call for renewal?

The answers to these questions are not my responsibility as a visitor and outsider, but no one should think that the challenges to freedom in today's world are easy, self-evident, or even congenial. The challenges are more difficult, arduous, and controversial than ever—and made even harder by the blanket of complacency and clichés with which Americans have smothered freedom. So, freedom's defense is never done. "Eternal vigilance is the price of liberty," we say, but we must never forget that such vigilance must be internal before it is external. The greatest dangers to freedom always come from within. We, whoever we are, are freedom's greatest enemy, so courage must always rise hand in hand with realism and humility.

WHAT DOES FREEDOM REQUIRE?

There will be no prediction here of any imminent American collapse. The abandonment of America's ordered freedom need not mean the immediate fall of America but only of the end of, first, the republic, and then of any meaningful democracy. America may continue powerful and wealthy for a while longer, but the reality is that more and more American ideals are breaking down or being exposed as a sham. And more and more Americans appear intent only on hedonism and the pursuit of their own pleasure and reliance on prosperity and technocracy to deliver dividends that virtue no longer strives for. Americans are either unsure of their distinctive ideals or openly cynical and dismissive about the way they have been set out recently. If this fatal drift runs its course, Americans will have carved into the chronicles of history yet another example of the failure of a free society and how the corruption of the best so easily becomes the worst.

All this raises urgent questions not only for Americans and admirers of the American republic but also for all who appreciate the ideal of ordered freedom. In the nineteenth century Søren Kierkegaard famously announced his ambition to "reintroduce Christianity into Christendom." Even at this late hour, it is urgent for Americans to reintroduce the first principles of freedom into the land of the free—to proclaim what those first principles are and to join hands with all those around the world who are striving to resist tyranny and to build their own free communities regardless of what happens to freedom in the one-time, self-proclaimed "empire of liberty."

Socrates famously called for an "examined life" and pronounced the unexamined life not worth living. Is there a national equivalent of the examined life, and is the present generation of Americans ready to face the findings of such a moral and historical testing? History is now presenting an ultimatum to America over freedom as the four questions already asked boil down to one essential question: *If Americans wish to continue as the land of the free, will they recognize the intrinsic character of freedom and respond to freedom as freedom itself requires, or will they continue to follow faulty and specious views of freedom and remain satisfied with their distortions and imitations until they suffer irreversible decline?* The period America is now entering represents *zero hour* for the American republic and its freedom. It calls for a grand historical decision and then a decisive *reset* and a *starting all over* that are not merely current fashionable slogans but genuine national repentance and about-face. Such decisive about-faces are rare in history, especially for a superpower still at the height of its dominance. But if America is not to decline as other nations have at a similar point, nothing less than the highest resolve and the wisest, most far-sighted, and determined response will be required. The normal run and rules of history are clear, but for people who know and respect freedom, freedom is never fate. For free people to-morrow can be different from yesterday and today. The future is open, not fixed, and America's choice between re-storing America's freedom and continuing America's decline is now.

2

UNDER OUR OWN VINE AND FIG TREE

THERE IS NEVER a wrong moment to celebrate and defend freedom. The times may be out of joint, but this book is for those who remain passionate about freedom and are committed to striving for freedom, not just for themselves but also for others. This is an invitation to explore the present crisis of freedom through what might seem a highly unlikely source: America's first president, George Washington. Washington not only coined the term "the great experiment" in freedom, but he had his own special picture of the ideal of freedom—his vision of citizens and communities living freely "under their own vine and fig tree." Washington is often called America's "indispensable man" and for a good reason. He is described this way because of the nobility of his character and the strength of his leadership rather than the importance of his thinking. Indeed, some have attributed many of his best ideas to his brilliantly gifted aide Alexander Hamilton. Be that as it may, America's present crisis, which unless it is resolved may well be terminal for the republic as it was founded, can be addressed constructively through an ideal that is indisputably Washington's, one that moved him profoundly. An indispensable man and an unlikely vision.

Remarkably, George Washington referred to his ideal of citizens enjoying life "under their own vine and fig tree" no less than forty-eight times in his writing. The most famous was his address to the Hebrew Congregation in Newport, Rhode Island, in 1790, where his focus was on religious freedom as a foundation for peace. "May the children of the stock of Abraham who dwell in this land continue to merit and enjoy the goodwill of other citizens—while everyone shall sit in safety under his own vine and fig tree and there shall be none to make him afraid." The other references are scattered mainly through his letters, and they are surely the tip of the iceberg of his own reflection on the theme, not to speak of his use of the idea in countless unrecorded conversations. Washington was, of course, quoting from the Hebrew Scriptures, where the phrase recurs three times in this form (Micah 4:4; 1 Kings 4:25; Zechariah 3:10).

It would be fair to say that both the Bible's use of the picture and Washington's quotations are easy to miss or to mock, and many people have never given them serious thought. Either response is a mistake. Properly understood, the vision of each citizen and each family living freely under their own vine and fig tree is more than a beautiful metaphor, an idle dream, or a matter of wishful thinking. If taken seriously, it could offer a vital key to the restoration of America as a free republic and to other societies and smaller or larger communities across the world. But even short of that, the vision stands as the key to the challenge of striving for personal freedom and the building and sustaining of strong families and healthy communities wherever they are sought.

ESCAPISM AND AGRARIAN NOSTALGIA?

The vision of freedom under our own vine and fig tree would be easy to scorn. It is commonly dismissed in two ways: either because of its original source, the Bible, or because of the particular way Washington used the picture. The Bible may be the book that made the Western world, but in a secularist age it is commonly dismissed. Even some who prize the Bible highly regard the vision as purely messianic and unattainable here and now. They admit that the vision is beautiful and powerful, but as a messianic dream, they say, it is utopian and beyond our reach.

To be sure, when Washington quotes the Bible, he does not cite chapter and verse, though his inclusion of the phrase "and none shall make them afraid" suggests that he was referring to the prophet Micah. Micah's version is the fullest and most exalted expression of the vision, and like Zechariah's it is certainly messianic. The prophet looks forward to the great Day of the Lord when

> Each of them will sit under his vine
> And under his fig tree,
> with no one to make *them* afraid.

The vision is preceded by the much-quoted depiction of messianic peace:

> Then they will hammer their swords into plowshares
> And their spears into pruning hooks;
> Nation will not lift up sword against nation,
> And never again will they train for war. (Micah 4:3-4)

For all whose hearts have been stirred by the deep longings of Tommy Dorsey's great spiritual "There Will Be Peace in the Valley," the key word in its messianic vision is *someday*.

Yet Micah's version of the vision is not the only one in the Bible, and it needs to be complemented by the way the vision is used in other places. At the opposite extreme from the messianism of Micah (and Dorsey), the same words are used in the setting of judgment and destruction. "I will destroy her vines and fig trees," God says through the prophet Hosea (Hosea 2:12). But the most interesting example of the phrase comes from the high point of Israel's renown during the reign of King Solomon. Israel's power and prosperity under Solomon, and the king's own wealth and wisdom, were unmatched in the Near East. In commenting on the splendor of Solomon's coronation, his chronicler remarks on the unprecedented prosperity that the people of Israel enjoyed: they "*were* as numerous as the sand that is on the seashore in abundance; *they* were eating and drinking and rejoicing," and Solomon "had peace on all sides around about him" (1 Kings 4:20, 24). The chronicler then climaxes his glowing description of Israel's high noon: "So Judah and Israel lived in safety, every man under his vine and his fig tree . . . all the days of Solomon" (1 Kings 4:25).

The prophets Hosea, Micah, and Zechariah all lived in darker times than Solomon. Hosea saw the destruction of vines and fig trees, and Micah and Zechariah foresaw that the full and final fulfillment of the vision would only be achieved in the future and with outside help—a hope that is messianic. But overall, the use of the vision was not utopian. It had been substantially fulfilled in Solomon's time. Living free under our own vine and fig tree was both a messianic hope and a social and political ideal that was realistic and achievable. It would one day be fulfilled perfectly, but it had been done before, if imperfectly, and it could be done again. George Washington thought so too.

Other people dismiss Washington's particular use of the vision. It was simply an old man's dream of retirement, they say, and irrelevant to us. In Washington's case the dream was fueled by an understandable desire to return to Mount Vernon, its Potomac view, and the Virginia way of life that he loved (which, sadly, depended to a considerable extent on the presence of slaves). In his last year as president, he wrote, "I had rather be on my farm than be emperor of the world." Conjure up the same picture today, critics say, and it will only spell privilege, escapism, or agrarian nostalgia. Unquestionably, there are elements of Washington's vision that are unattainable in today's urban world and elements in his situation that were wrong. But it would be uncharitable not to allow for any negative elements in Washington's mind. A land surveyor since he was young, he must have longed to stop looking at other people's land and enjoy his own. As a general he had seen the ravages of war, and his heart must have ached for real peace. As a politician he had borne the heavy burdens of the new nation, and he was surely ready to hand over the reins to others and manage his own affairs.

All such negative reasons behind his vision were understandable, and doubtless we each have our own negative reasons to long for freedom and peace. But it would be wrong and even more uncharitable not to recognize the positive reasons behind Washington's dream too—reasons that went beyond the privileges of his glorious Potomac estate, the likes of which few of us will share. When Washington set out his vision for the Rhode Island synagogue, for example, the Jews he reassured in his letter had no slaves, they owned no large estates, and their own contrast to the vision was their horrendous experience of persecution and scattering in Europe. The truth is that in both the Bible's picture and in Washington's use of the picture, the vision of each citizen living freely under their own vine and fig tree meant much more than privilege and escape. *At its heart, it spoke of an ideal of freedom, independence, simplicity, work and its rewards, safety, peace, fruitfulness, contentment, freedom of conscience, and all in the setting of home and being local.*

The question we must ask is, are such aspects of freedom still attainable in the advanced and urbanized modern world, or are they beyond recall? And if they are, what does freedom require and how are we to build, sustain, or restore such freedom today? And how are we to extend the benefits and blessings of freedom to everyone and not just to a privileged elite who can literally live under their vine and fig tree and relax by their swimming pools in the Hamptons, Palm Beach, Beverly Hills, or Napa Valley? The fulfillment of that idea and its significance for freedom in the global era is the theme of this book.

NO POLITICAL
MASTERPIECE?

GIORGIO VASARI, the Renaissance architect, artist, and the father of art history and criticism, was a passionate admirer of Michelangelo. In particular he praised the great painter and sculptor for his use of dramatic, contrasting colors that were so different from the soft and muted harmonies used by his equally great contemporary Leonardo da Vinci. Vasari's insight pays dividends in areas far wider than Renaissance art. Context is essential for meaning, but contrast is a key to clarity. Similarly, the Bible's vision and Washington's dream come alive and stand out today when we understand them set over against certain troubling features of our advanced modern world. Three major factors provide such clarity of contrast—and urgency. They demonstrate why this vision of personal, local, and community freedom is so important today. It is neither the sole nor the sufficient way to pursue freedom, but it is a necessary way because it balances other extremes and counters other pitfalls.

Contrast is the mother of clarity, and the ideal of living under our own vine and fig tree shines brighter and becomes more urgent in light of these alternatives and their deficiencies. In that sense, the vision of the vine and fig tree matters to citizens in every free society, from the humblest to the highest in the land.

THE BEST REGIME FOR EVERYONE EVERYWHERE?

Washington's vision speaks to the heart of one of humanity's greatest questions in the global era: Is it possible in the advanced modern world to create societies that do justice to the worth of each human being and create communities with freedom, equality, justice, stability, and peace for all? Many people, it appears, live and think as if that ideal is only a pipe dream now and an idyllic dream from earlier, simpler times. But if it is considered possible, what would it mean in practice, and by what authority should its foundational principles of the vision be affirmed—based on reason or nature or history or evolution or—as with Washington's vision from the Bible—by faith in God?

That search for a vision of the good community and a free commonwealth is framed and made urgent by the fact that political bookends of history are authoritarianism and anarchy, Caesarism and chaos, Big Brother and the prodigal son, the iron heel and the unencumbered self, or order-with-no-freedom at one extreme and freedom-with-no-order at the other. The two extremes not only serve to counter each other but to reinforce each other. Since anarchy is less livable and even more destructive than authoritarianism, humans prefer tyranny to anarchy. Get too close to Thomas Hobbes's "war of all against all" and the lure of Leviathan becomes irresistible.

Post–World War I Weimar was the perfect slipway for Hitler, just as the war-torn ravages and corruptions of twentieth-century China made even Mao Zedong a relief, for a while. And as the names Hitler and Mao make clear, authoritarianism in the advanced modern world almost certainly means totalitarianism. Better submit to control than suffer chaos. If such dynamics are in play at the extremes, the challenge is to build the good community by creating and sustaining a vision of ordered freedom that avoids the two extremes, that demonstrates a constructive alternative for humanity, and that guarantees personal and communal freedom at its heart.

Many people lament that the question is even harder to answer today because the age-old search for the "best regime for everyone everywhere" has foundered. It has indeed, but let's be clear: the failure of that search is a good thing. True, no candidate can now make that claim to be the best with assurance, not even democracy and the ideal of representative government (which was the occasion for Winston Churchill's wry comment, "Democracy is the worst system devised by the wit of man, except for all the others"). But importantly, other candidates such as socialism and communism that once boasted they were history's answer have only stoked the fear that in the global era any proposed answer could be imposed on the entire world now, whether people want it or not. In the name, say, of a New World Order, such a vision would be a contradiction of freedom from the outset.

The truth is that over the past two centuries much Western thinking about freedom, including much American thought, has given up on the answers put forward in succession by reason, by nature, by history, and by evolution, just as many had abandoned their faith in God earlier. That negative conclusion is easily and quickly stated, but we need to weigh the gravity of rejecting all such answers and then concluding only in the negative—in despair.

Can any of those five answers—reason, nature, history, evolution, or faith in God—provide a foundation for freedom and free societies, or must we face the fact that no such foundation is conceivable and the very vision is impossible? That is a weighty question for humanity and the human future. Without a solid answer that justifies freedom, the alternative prospects for humanity are reliance on technique, force, nihilism, authoritarianism, and endless variations on power and the brutal abuse of some humans by other humans. In short, it would mean the world of the radical and revolutionary left that we have witnessed in a thousand forms since 1789, the world in which revolutions never work and oppression never ends.

This striving toward an ideal politics and the search for the best regime for everyone everywhere have been at the heart of the West ever since Socrates and Plato, and at the heart of the modern world for five hundred years. They have come to a head in our time. Following the rise of the modern world and the influence of the Renaissance, the Protestant Reformation, and the Catholic Reformation, the human masterpieces created in Western art, literature, music, and science have been prodigious and enduring—by Dante,

Leonardo, Michelangelo, William Shakespeare, Francis Bacon, Johann Sebastian Bach, Isaac Newton, Rembrandt, and their successors. But for all the many attempts, from Machiavelli to Marx, John Stuart Mill, and John Rawls, *the West has produced no equivalent political masterpiece.*

Indeed, history is littered with the ruins of failed attempts. Ironically, the greatest menace to the West today is posed by the West's political exports to Asia: the totalitarianism of Karl Marx and the drive to the homogeneity of Carl Schmitt in China, which to the chagrin of China's traditional patriots are as European as they come. The irony is unmistakable. The West is in decline, but from one side Western ideas are rising to rule the world from Asia, and from another they supply the chief weapons assaulting the West from within the West.

But the failed and fallible political models go far further back. For one thing, the classical forms of government—monarchy, aristocracy, and democracy—have all provided copious illustrations of their corrupt and failed variations, just as the Greeks and Romans warned. For another, the more modern ideologies—such as democracy, liberalism, socialism, nationalism, communism, and fascism—have each betrayed their supporters' hopes in their turn. Hence the present question: Is it still possible to create and sustain societies that, even in some imperfect way, could be described as masterpieces of political wisdom, realism, freedom, hope—and humanity? And are we aware of the benefits and realistic about the shortcomings of each model, especially the one we choose to adopt?

It was once thought that the American republic offered strong prospects of the high ideals of ordered freedom, building from a rocklike assurance of personal freedom. But for all the daring and brilliance of the founding generation, for all the ransacked lessons of history, and for all the ingenious devices designed to counter the abuse of power, America's great experiment in freedom is proving to be no masterpiece either. From the very start Americans ought to have been as vigilant about the weaknesses of their model as they were jubilant about its strengths, but sadly the rejoicing outstripped the realism, and the vulnerability has been exposed. With the weaknesses plain to see, America's intelligentsia now routinely repudiate the foundations that made the republic what it was intended to be, and the present generation of Americans now appears bent on squandering the hard-won lessons of the long history of freedom.

Worse still, authoritarianism is growing apace in America. From the campus censoring of speech and the cancel culture to the insistence that it is right and necessary for government and big tech to police speech, to the overwhelming trust in and reliance on the national security apparatus despite decades of abuse, to the abuse of courts to allow spying on citizens, to the harassing of citizens through solitary confinement without trial, to the opening of almost all private bank accounts to government scrutiny, there are incontrovertible signs of growing American authoritarianism in attitudes and actions. The culture wars rage on, and the eventual victors will be the last ones standing with all the remaining power in their hands. That will be the moment to see who holds the imperial purple of the new Caesar or the mantle of the new Bonaparte.

History bulges with examples of authoritarianism from both the right and the left, and both extremes will always be a danger. The Caesar, the emperor, the führer, the party chairman, the president for life, the iron heel, and the Big Brother will be no surprise to those who have read Jacob Burckhardt, Fyodor Dostoevsky, Aldous Huxley, George Orwell, and many other writers and their warnings. Which is the greater threat in America is for history to show, but there is no question that the present authoritarian trends are clearer and politically stronger on the left than the right—if only because of their greater power and the prestige of their social location.

For all the extreme ugliness and undoubted menace of the right, it cannot match the left for its presence in and favors from the government, the deep state, the academy, the intelligence community, the press and media, and woke business and woke capital. The last two are especially vital to the left. Once considered the last redoubt of conservative America, business is both the most surprising scalp of the radical left and one of the most important captures because of the direct impact of banks and corporations on daily American consumer life.

When Fortune 500 companies and their human resources departments march to the tune of the Southern Poverty Law Center in discerning what is hate, when banks without any notice can suddenly withdraw the credit cards of groups they do not approve of, when major corporations fawn over the Black Lives Matter leaders, and when the idea of stakeholder capitalism is stretched elastically to include any category of approved victims as the stakeholders du jour, it is clear that the radical revolution has made spectacular headway and has done so with most Americans oblivious to the sounding death knell of the republic.

Ironically, America's proto-authoritarians in the political sphere are blind to their creeping authoritarianism. They now march forward under the banner of doing all they do "to save democracy" from their opponents. Is this a matter of hypocrisy or projection? They constantly cite the very evident splinter in Donald Trump's eye, but conveniently ignore the hefty log in their own as they strive to manipulate the Constitution and consolidate power beyond anything their forebears could have hoped to achieve. One-party faculty clubs, one-party newsrooms, and one-party states such as California signal the menace of the prospect of one-party national politics that, for the moment, comes from one side only.

REVOLUTION, OLIGARCHY, OR HOMECOMING?

The choice Americans have created for themselves today can be stated simply: *Revolution, Oligarchy,* or *Homecoming*? The revolution option represents the choice offered by revolutionary liberationism or the radical left of neo-Marxism or cultural Marxism that is so powerful among the intelligentsia and the cultural gatekeepers of America. The oligarchy option represents the degeneration of American politics caused by the hollowing out of traditional liberalism and the consolidation of its newly illiberal politics with the bureaucratic state and its expertise, with the national security state, the press and the media, the academy, entertainment, woke finance and business, and hi-tech—all together undermining all separation of powers, thus creating the menace of one-party national politics and government by the elite, the powerful, and the wealthy: in short, the ruling class or the rulers and the ruled, the controllers and the controlled, and the subversion of genuine democracy by oligarchy. The homecoming option represents the vision of a Lincoln-like "new birth of freedom," in the sense of the Hebrew word for repentance, *teshuvah*, which means not only a radical change of heart and mind but a return from alienation and exile and therefore a homecoming to what made America great in the first place.

Let there be no misunderstanding. The vision of the vine and fig is a humble vision. Not for a moment does it presume to be either a one-size-fits-all political solution for the world or a blueprint for the best regime for everyone everywhere. On the contrary it is the antidote to such monstrosities. What it provides are the components for the local end of any broader political model that would stand against the menace of the one-size-fits-all solutions of globalism. As a celebration of local particularity and diversity, the vision of the vine and fig is the complete and absolute antithesis of all attempts at uniformity and conformity and a perfect counterbalance to the benefits of the properly global. The natural diversity of the world is too rich for political uniformity, and contrary to socialism, communism, and authoritarianism, freedom rules out any attempt at enforced conformity. A globalist bid to build a political order for everyone everywhere would be an architectural plan for a global Tower of Babel. It would be Big Brother authoritarianism and totalitarianism on a monstrous and forbidding scale, and it must be resisted by all who love freedom.

The key to the vision of citizens under their vine and fig tree is the particularity of each community's uniqueness, history, and values and the expression of this commitment blended with universal and enduring principles of freedom. It is therefore a vision for those who know themselves and their story and who understand their vision and freely commit themselves to continue it. For Jews and Americans it would certainly be a homecoming in that it reflects the best of the principles at the heart of their respective founding (from which each has strayed significantly). But the vision has much to offer to families, to communities, and to people all around the world who are willing to explore its way of building a commonwealth of freedom, large or small, based on human dignity, freedom, justice, peace, and stability.

THE COMPLETEST
REVOLUTION OF ALL?

ANOTHER CONSIDERATION THAT heightens the importance of Washington's vision is that it addresses the heart of one of America's deepest crises. Rabbi Jonathan Sacks called this problem "cultural climate change," a change that will prove even more menacing to freedom and humanity than climate change—though given far less attention. Climate change is important because it is all about our human relationship to things that are immediate though external to us, such as the damage to nature and the depletion of the earth's resources we depend on. Cultural climate change is even more important, as we are beginning to appreciate, because it affects the even more damaging exhaustion of our personal resources and our inner energies as individual human beings. In the first case, our science, our technology, and our visions of progress are the villains, but in the second case they are the masks that prevent us from seeing what we are doing not to nature but to our own selves.

More than a century ago Lord James Bryce warned of this core crisis toward the end of his magisterial *The American Commonwealth*. Second only to Alexis de Tocqueville as a foreign commentator on the United States, he mused on a striking difference between Europe and America. Whatever its spiritual and moral state, Europe at the time (around AD 1900) had both tradition and the social cohesion of small towns and villages to hold it together. As a rapidly developing young country, America had neither tradition nor any natural social cohesion. Indeed, America was free and on the move to a degree that Europe could only dream of. Its motto might well have been "Move on! Move on!" Only one thing held America together amid such freedom, mobility, and change—religion.

Flourishing because of the First Amendment and disestablishment, not in spite of it, religion in America around 1900 was massive in its solidity and influence. Tocqueville had described religion in the 1830s as "the first of the political institutions" in America. To most people at the time it was unthinkable that religion might ever not be what it was then. However, Bryce mused, if religion in America were ever to lose its strength and authority, the result would be "the completest revolution of all." The strongest bonding in American society would have gone, and unbounded freedom would run amok and work to cause its own undoing.

Call Bryce's revolution *erosion, fraying, unraveling, ungluing*, or whatever term you choose, but it is the deep crisis that is undermining America today. America has scrambled the spelling of the key adjective in its name, and the United States has become the "Untied" States (and disintegrating communities). Put simply, America's *philosophical cynicism, moral corruption*, and *social collapse* have caused a massive crisis of faith and trust and an erosion of freedom that form the cultural climate change and the completest revolution at the core of American culture today. Will America's brave new elites wake up to this new and even more dangerous threat? This profound cultural disaster lies upstream from all the political decisions, legal disputes, economic trends, and election results that grab the daily headlines of our attention, and it is far more important than any of them. The erosion begins in ideas and undermines the foundations of truth, trustworthiness, trust, promise-keeping, loyalty, allegiance—and freedom. Left unattended, the decay of truth and trust spells the ruin of the republic.

SUSPECT THY NEIGHBOR AS THYSELF

Why *philosophical cynicism*? At our best we humans are seekers after truth—in our faiths and philosophies of life, our academic pursuits, our scientific explorations, and our journalism. But this aspiration is now being choked off, and with it our humanity is debased. Philosophy is essentially the pursuit of wisdom through thinking about thinking, so that good and bad philosophy are good and bad thinking about thinking. Today's philosophical cynicism comes from the fact that much of the American (and European) academy has become a giant shredding machine. Its skepticism has undermined all confidence in notions such as truth, moral knowledge, objective reality, and meaning. At the highest academic level the concept of truth has been savaged by postmodernism and deconstruction.

Like an unfortunate person caught in a revolving door spinning so fast they cannot get out, the devotees (or victims) of postmodernism are whirling around and around in a world of radical indeterminacy, chronic undecidability, and endless uncertainty and anxiety. Speakers have no authority over what they are saying, nor authors over the meaning of what they have written, and listeners and readers can never rest in what they take as meaning. There is no definitive meaning for anything and no stopping point for possible interpretations and reinterpretations.

This situation is now triply disastrous. First and most important, the crisis of truth means that everything, absolutely everything is undecidable. Second, we are told, not only is nothing clear any longer but no one and nothing is without subterranean motives and agendas. After all, if truth is dead and all that is left is power, then as Glaucon argued in Plato's *Republic,* justice is "whatever is in the interests of the stronger party." Then too, as Lenin stated, the only questions are Who? Whom? (Who has the power, and over whom?) This means that we mustn't just read or listen to what is being said but interrogate it, armed with our own suspicion and ever alert for the phony being passed off on us and the power agenda behind it. George Orwell saw this danger clearly in the revolutionary left of his day. In his famous novel *1984,* O'Brien states frankly, "The Party seeks power entirely for its own sake. . . . The object of power is power." In the postmodern world this brazen preoccupation with power touches everybody, even those who do not agree with it but are its victims if all knowledge is only power. The result is a citizenry with suspicion as its worldview.

Third, to make matters worse the whole approach is expressed in the impenetrable jargon of the initiated. (Most of us have a common cold from time to time, but a postmodernist, it is said, suffers from "vasomotor rhinitis.") The full outcome of this disastrous philosophy is that there is no truth, there is only radical relativism and endless interpretations, and thus a myriad of personal truths—my truth, your truth, her truth, his truth, their truth. Nothing is what it appears to be, so only suspicion can unlock the real motive below the surface and decipher the obscurantism.

At best, every interpretation is at once a misinterpretation, a rival interpretation, and an automatic invitation to respond with suspicion, disagreement, and relentless debunking. With no solid truth, those who have influence can only wield power, and their power plays easily become a form of critical terrorism to all other interpretations. The immediate effect of postmodernism is a crazy quilt patchwork of Oprah Winfrey–style personal truths, but the ultimate result is a society that is intellectually on the edge of a nervous breakdown and fogbound and becalmed in confusion, suspicion, conflict, terminal uncertainty—and power-mongering.

For anyone who understands freedom, it is simply inescapable that freedom requires truth, a shared sense of truth, and therefore trustworthiness and trust. George Orwell's *1984* is the classical warning against the danger of denying truth and objective reality. In the ringing line of Aleksandr Solzhenitsyn's Nobel Address, "one word of truth outweighs

the world." Yet to take a stand against the postmodern
chorus and insist on objective *truth* in today's cultural
climate is to be considered authoritarian, to court being dismissed as fascist, and to be abused by the Big Brother consensus like Orwell's Winston Smith. As in *1984*, so today: war
is peace, slavery is freedom, error is truth, evil is good, and
if they say so, men are women and women are men.

At the more popular level, American freedom has been battered by wave after wave of relativism (there is no objective
truth), followed by emotivism (truth is whatever you feel to
be true), historicism (each age and now each generation is
shaped by its own truth), and then constructivism ("truth" is
socially constructed according to what we all together take
to be true or make to be true). Yet postmodernism speaks out
of both sides of its mouth. It offers relativism as a universal
entitlement: "Everyone is entitled to their own truth, so your
truth is as good as anyone else's truth." But then comes the
catch. Postmodernism is also all about power, and therefore
the powerful. So, to paraphrase Orwell. "All truths are equal,
but some truths are more equal than others."

The practical and rather obvious result of such a rejection
of truth is vulnerability to lies, falsehoods, rumors, delusions,
and chronic suspicion of everyone and everything. In terms
of the sexual revolution every man must now be seen as
every woman's potential assailant and every woman as every
man's potential accuser. In terms of the political revolution,
every authority is now a potential tyrant and every citizen a
potential rebel (and now domestic terrorist).

With the excesses of the gender revolution the revolt
against terms and categories becomes a revolt against

reality, and all the rest of us are pressured to deny the obvious, believe in the incredible, and go along with the charade of the emperor's new clothes. ("Only a woman can get pregnant," but such truisms are now held to be false and offensive.) Unsurprisingly, the outcome of the blend of postmodernism and cultural Marxism is a deep crisis of faith and trust, opening up a vulnerability to cynicism, suspicion, and mistrust, and then to nihilism and power-mongering. What else could be the result of two centuries of doubting, deriding, deconstructing, debasing, and defiling everything once considered important or normal?

When Israel's celebrated foreign secretary Abba Eban received an award from his alma mater, Cambridge University, he began his response with a smile, "It was here that I learned the honesty, integrity, and love of truth that have been such a disadvantage to me in my political career." That quip would fall flat today when the triumph of postmodernism offers the perfect courses for anyone wanting to be schooled in the lies, hype, and spin that are the currency of modern politics. Needless to say, few postmodernists live by their own standards. No text has decidable meaning, our brave new professors say, but woe betide the reviewer who misunderstands what the postmodern scholars write in their books. As Walker Percy quipped, the postmodernist is an academic who tells you that texts have no clear meaning but who leaves a precise message on his wife's answering machine requesting a pepperoni pizza for supper.

But the effect is worse than trivial hypocrisy. Humanity itself is degraded. We are no longer capable of aspiring to be seekers after truth, even as we recognize the perils of self-deception.

We are now condemned to be no more than chronic liars, in-veterate hypocrites, rationalizers, and ideologists—those whose ideas are always and inevitably smokescreens for their personal impulses and interests, or whose ideas simply serve their social institutions. People who don't realize this fact are simpletons. Those who do and aim to make the most of it are cynics or opportunists. For those who follow Nietzsche all roads lead to antitruth and to power. In short, the triumph of trends such as positivism, materialism, postmodernism, and critical theory is a grand intellectual monument to the decline and defeat of truth in America, and together they deliver a body blow to freedom in the land of the free.

Truth has died in key parts of America, and lies, delusions, and chaotic lifestyles of all kinds are run-of-the-mill throughout the land. With no commanding truths left to be-lieve and to obey except under the authority of the self and the state, America since the 1960s has slid into a deep crisis of cultural authority. The "Thou shalt nots" of Moses have melted and the "You have heard it said, but I say unto you" of Jesus has evaporated. When a once-free nation breeds intel-lectuals whose thinking is an all-out assault on the nation's foundational ideas, and these same intellectuals operate as the nation's thought police, the result can only be the suicide of a free people.

Today, as postmodernism wreaks its havoc on America, there will soon be nothing sacred, nothing true, nothing good, and nothing certain left. Then tomorrow, without the sacred, the true, the good, and the solidly certain, there will be little left of America as America has been. And worse, there will be vulnerability to the creators and controllers of the metaverse. Postmodernism deconstructs and the metaverse will reconstruct. But as ever when realities are imagined and reimagined, constructed, deconstructed, and reconstructed, the sole principle in play will be power, and the sole question will be who controls the controllers.

WHO'S TO SAY WHAT'S RIGHT IN HUMPTY DUMPTY LAND

The *moral corruption* follows naturally, and it stems from the impact of philosophical cynicism on ordinary thinking and daily behavior. Where God is held to be dead—and postmodernism is alive and well—everything is permitted *so long as you can get away with it and you can hire a good lawyer.* The result of such a rejection of objectivity, truth, and morality is vulnerability to confusion, suspicion, mistrust, and manipulation. The abuse of truth starts in theory, but it finds its perfect partner in technology and technique. Together, they start as a form of radical social constructionism—there are no givens, either from creation or natural law, so everything can be constructed, deconstructed, and reconstructed at will, all in accordance with the fashion of the day. This leads to the abuse of words, which leads in turn to an abuse of speech and images and then to turning society into a hall of mirrors made of falsehood, unreality, and illusion. The poison of the medium-is-the-message impact of social media is obvious, but the crisis of the deepfake world is deeper and more damaging.

When truth in journalism is a relic and there is no difference between news and fake news, how are citizens to trust what they see or hear? The mainstream press awarded

President Trump many Pinocchios for his false statements. But a year after he left office, one report after another showed how the same press's "assured narratives" of his misdoings such as Russiagate were entirely false—though they were published as consensus truths and peddled by national leaders and once-respectable outlets such as the *New York Times*, CNN, and MSNBC. Not only that, the false narratives were planted carefully by politicians and reaffirmed solemnly by leaders of the intelligence community, and they were rewarded with Pulitzer Prizes, which were not rescinded even when the reporting was exposed as false. President Trump was no choir boy, but the brazen assault on truth by America's mainstream press was evident in the brazenly biased reporting on Trump and the equally egregious pass given to the Biden family over its own multiple scandals and its influence peddling.

Thanks to postmodernism and hi-tech, who is now to say what is true or false, right or wrong, good or bad, trustworthy or dubious? The very categories are discredited at the personal level, and the problems multiply. For example, even so-called fact checkers have been exposed for their bias and selective vision. Or again, the fashionable notion of authenticity, "To thine own self be true," has been shown up as empty. It has become fashionable at the very moment when, without truth, it is vacuous, fluid, and manipulable.

How are we to tell the difference between the authentic and the fake without truth? The problem touches on the current ban on cultural appropriation in acting. Truth and authenticity are said to prohibit actors from acting as anyone from a different nationality or race. So, no Englishman can play Othello, a Moor, and almost no African or Asian can take the part of Shylock, a Jew. Shakespeare himself would be canceled. Yet by the very same principle of authenticity, transgenderism encourages men to "follow their truth" and believe they have become women, and women to believe they have become men.

Thus, bizarrely, as British journalist Melanie Phillips notes, "Authenticity has become mandatory in fiction and while imagination has become mandatory in real life." In short, in the looking-glass wonderland of postmodernism and the sexual revolution "living your truth" has become another word for living a lie. To this point the emperor still struts around in the nude, and there are enough fawning courtiers from the academy and the media to silence the mirth of the small boy who sees the truth all too clearly. Future generations will have to decide whether such pretenses are a matter of make-believe, stupidity, insanity, or simply the lengths to which the revolutionaries must go in their assault on objective truth and all givens.

Questions are thrusting out at the public level too. Is honest government and honest journalism still possible? Can any official statements or news reports be taken seriously at face value? What are responsible citizens to do in such a climate of lies and half-truths? At best everything is contested, contentious, suspect, and a matter of who has the power to say something and to make it stick. At worst things are upside down, inside out, and literally unreal. Nothing is good or bad in itself. What was considered true is now viewed as false, what was wrong can now be made to look right. Objective morality has died in America, and Americans are living in Humpty Dumpty land with no truth to steady them and provide them bearings. Technique on the one hand and perversity on the other are now run-of-the-mill throughout the land. Freedom has become impossible.

For all the mind-spinning disputes surrounding the notion of truth, the notion of truth is important because truth is inescapably a matter of reality. Contrary to the modern idea that truth only exists in the minds of the people who believe in it, truth has an objective dimension. Put simply, *if something is true or false, its truth or falsehood is a claim about something, and what truth is about is nothing less than the reality of reality*. Lying is therefore an intention to deceive that creates an alternative reality—or falsehood and *unreality*. A culture of lying fosters delusions, undermines freedom, distorts justice, blacklists disagreements and debate, and poisons society. Lying is not only the enemy of truth, it is the enemy of humanity and freedom. Words not only create worlds, but they also destroy worlds. When words are, first, belittled, emptied, and reduced to "words, words, words," whether by advertisers or by polished public liars, they are no longer commitments and they no longer serve reality. Then, when words are used only as weapons, weaponized words become instruments of power and hypocrisy as well as violence. The same people who boast of their politics of rights are the very ones whose attacks on others or censorship of others is an assertion of force and a degradation of rights—for as their behavior demonstrates, those who have no power have no rights, no recourse, and no redress.

In short, when truth dies, all that is left is lies, delusion, and force, and when truth and words break down, abuse, violence, and authoritarianism are at the door. Mr. President, Madam Speaker, Members of the House and Senate, owners and editors of the mainstream press and media, and executives of Google and Facebook, consider your ways. The great American experiment cannot survive your carelessness, your delinquency, or your plain mendacity.

THE GREAT MELTDOWN

The third element of the crisis, *social collapse*, comes from the combined impact of philosophical cynicism and moral corruption on the ties that bind society together. Many other factors have been cited over the years. As far back as the 1960s, for example, supporters of the traditional family feared that it would be undone by a trio of assaults—free love, easy divorce, and abortion. Since then the impact of those factors has been compounded by the onslaught of the sexual revolutionaries, whether early dreamers such as the Marquis de Sade, grand strategists such as Wilhelm Reich, or individual radicals such as the writer Philip Roth and the filmmaker Woody Allen. (Anyone who doubts this statement need only read the memoirs written over against them by their wives, Claire Bloom and Mia Farrow.)

Yet the invisible crisis of the completest revolution lies even deeper than all of the different individuals who have contributed to it. Without a solid grasp of truth, an accepted notion of right and wrong, and the implicit commitment of the use of words, the core bonding of all American relationships is eroding. Decades such as the 1960s, with its moral revolution and its open counterculture, highlighted the cultural climate change and the completest revolution with undeniable force, but there is no escaping the longer and wider trends. The grand unraveling has eroded the three institutions that are the bedrock of the freedom of the republic—families, schools, and churches and synagogues. It touches atheists no less than Catholics and Mormons. It corrodes the marriages and families of Muslims and not only Evangelicals. It reduces children to economic factors and bringing them into the world to a calculation of pros and cons, with the birth rate showing a clear and growing bias toward the cons. If there is no truth to negotiate the differences between reality and unreality, no ties to bind, no loyalty to any loyalties, and no North Pole to pull back the compasses to true north, then the completest revolution becomes impossible to stop and the great American experiment in freedom is doomed. In the words of one congressman, "If there is a flood, a small boy can put his finger in the dike and become a hero, but what I see in America is a mudslide."

Wake up, America. The trends are coming together and piling up. The day is coming when no clear ethics are known or taught, self-restraint is overwhelmed by consumerism, conscience is silenced by correctness, the moral knowledge that was the capital of the past runs out, and the metaverse deepens the confusion between the real and the virtual. Reality itself will then deliver its bill. The penalty exacted for the sins of American slavery has been crippling enough. What is coming is a devastation of even greater proportions, a moral dust bowl, a carnival of identity confusions, and a hall of mirrors of reality distortions—all brought on by the unaddressed cultural climate change.

What will survive when the college-bred locusts of doubt, derision, deconstruction, and deception have done their work? When everything simple, natural, normal, traditional, genuine, and honest has been pulled down? No one will be sure of reality or understand who they are and what they are about with any assurance. All will be manipulable, only the few will hold the strings, and whatever moral criteria they choose will be the commanding consensus. Personal freedom, self-government, covenantal republicanism, and representative democracy will have been ruined beyond recall.

For those with eyes to see, the coronavirus pandemic stands as a warning to America. The plague was a trailer for the crisis that will come if the nation persists in its present course. The virus made nonsense of human control. The credibility of science was undermined by its own scientific experts. Political power grabs became obvious. Factions and clashing opinions multiplied. Ordinary people mistrusted leaders, and leaders were exasperated by ordinary people. Future economic and educational prospects were blighted for many. And above all, the general fatigue and anxiety deepened into a crisis of faith and mental health that broke out in widespread depression, disruptive behavior, breakdown, and suicides.

Once again, we are not talking about the short term, and history has no inevitability. The United States may continue for a while as a strong, wealthy, advanced modern nation, but it must soon give up any pretense of being the land of the free. That is the danger of the crisis of truth and trust in America. Where there is high truth in society, there can be high trust, and where there is high trust, there can be high freedom. But where there is low truth and low trust, there will have to be high control and a resort to either surveillance ("I trust them no further than I can see them") or to tribalism ("I can only trust people and news from people like me").

When mistrust is the default philosophy and suspicion the best insurance against being fooled, the rot spreads through society fast. Citizens grow wary of their fellow citizens, they mistrust experts and journalists and political leaders, and they will have little trust in their institutions and even in science wielded as the power tool of the elites. The outcome can only be a dangerous rise of tension, suspicion, anger, and endless conflicts of power—and a serious degrading of freedom. Without truth there is only power (a.k.a. force), and for those with no power, there is no right and no rights. The same blunt conclusion becomes plastered all over America at point after point: without truth there can be no freedom.

The elite disdains the deplorables for their conspiracy theories and disinformation, and the deplorables mistrust the elite for their fake news and their censorship of all they disagree with, but both accusations can be laid at the door of the philosophical cynicism that underlies them all. Let no one fool themselves: just as happened to poor George Floyd in Minneapolis in 2020, America's intelligentsia has knelt on the neck of truth and stifled American freedom so that it cannot breathe and soon will die. The soft authoritarianism and one-party politics of the oligarchy are already making a mockery of both the founders' covenantal republicanism and of Lincolnian democracy and representative government.

The deep irony, of course, is that President Macron of France and other European leaders are now warning their people against the menace of corrosive ideas coming from American universities, when the origin of the ideas is the very country, France, now raising the alarm.

There is always a link between the vitality of a nation and the vitality of its predominant philosophy, and that fact spells trouble for America. Good philosophy means good thinking about the major questions of life, so today's cultural climate change spells stormy weather and hazardous times ahead for America.

The vision of living freely under our own vine and fig tree, with its sturdy philosophy and robust ethics, stands in direct opposition to this clear and present danger. The only question is whether there is a will to explore and to apply its remedy while there is still time.

5

AN OFFSET FOR
THE RESET?

YET ANOTHER REASON for the urgency of exploring
Washington's vision of the vine and fig is that it counters
a fatal temptation at the heart of globalization, one that is
currently promoted fervently by one side and feared equally
fervently by the other. This is the temptation of the globalist
vision of the New World Order to be achieved through such
means as H. G. Wells's vision of a "World Republic," Klaus
Schwab's Davos call for a post-pandemic "Global Reset"
(now rebranded as "the great narrative"), George Soros's su-
perfunding of a borderless world, and John Lennon's
dreaming in "Imagine." To do justice to this vision and to the
responses it has stirred, we must hold two things in mind.
First, we must remember the inherent human tensions between the universal and the particular, the global and the
local, the world and the parish, and between our far-reaching
minds and our physically limited human bodies. Second, we

must distinguish the process of globalization from the philosophy of globalism.

Globalization is simply the process by which human interconnectedness has expanded to a truly global level. As such, globalization is incontestable and far from new. It can be traced back to the march of conquering armies and the spread of empires, though it advanced enormously through such breakthroughs as Roman roads, Portuguese sailing ships, British steam engines, and modern jet airplanes. It has now expanded exponentially again through modern telecommunications and the "three S factors" (their speed, scale, and simultaneity). Thus, today we can travel almost everywhere in the world in a few hours, and we can communicate almost everywhere in real-time. Unquestionably, the power and importance of globalization are here to stay. The basic challenge with the process of globalization is how to describe it accurately and comprehensively before responding to it. For better or worse, it is here to stay. To ignore it would be foolish, and to resist it would be futile.

The *philosophy of globalism* is quite different. Globalism is "the worldview of those who recognize the significance of the process of globalization, and wish to take advantage of it, and to do so by exploiting the global at the expense of the local, and the world at the expense of the parish." As such it is questionable and anything but incontestable. The biologist René Dubos was famous for his maxim, "Think globally, act locally," but that balance is highly demanding and not as simple as it sounds. In America, for example, the word *federal* comes from the Latin *foedus*, for "covenant." The federal system was originally intended to be an agreed pact and a covenantal partnership between the nation's capital and the states and thus between the national and the local, the US Congress and the local town hall, safeguarding both unity and diversity. The objective was a wise separation of powers (or checks and balances) as the means to counter the potential abuse of concentrated power at the nation's center. Today, however, the connotation of *federal* and the *feds* has changed beyond recognition. Federal and the feds are all about Washington and not the states, the central and not the local, and thus the coercive and not the covenantal, the imposed and not the independent and freely agreed.

The unfortunate fact is that as globalization expands, the balance between the global and the local becomes ever more strained and lopsided in favor of the global. *National* was once considered a threat to the local, but today the global poses a threat to both the national and the local. The global advances and strengthens, leapfrogging even the national, while the truly local stands still, steadily shrinking in importance and appearing more and more quaint and rundown. Nationalism, for example, has been divorced from patriotism and branded as irredeemably negative. The easiest and the most profitable response is to ignore the balance, just as the globalists propose—in other words, to stress the new at the expense of the old, to exploit the new global reality at the expense of the old national and local reality and so to go with the flow and let the devil take the hindmost.

In sum, the easy way forward is to advance authoritarianism and suppress freedom. Before the rise of the modern world it was rare for most people to travel very far and thus easy to treat the local with the seriousness it deserved. The place where people were born was the place where they lived and died. When my wife and I lived in Switzerland, we had neighbors who had never been more than a mile up the road to the next village. Today, of course, few people now live the way that most people lived once. In contrast to my Swiss neighbors, I was born on one continent, I was educated in another, I am now living in yet another, and I have visited most of the major countries in the world—a story that is far from rare.

IF IT CAN BE DONE, IT WILL BE

Yet the challenge lies deeper still. Not only is it hard to keep the balance between the global and the local, but it is more profitable not to try. The lure of the new and ever more global, promises profit as well as power. After all, as Jacques Ellul stressed with the advances of technology: if something can be done, it will be done, and if we don't do it, someone else will. The globalists openly favor the new over the old, the global at the expense of the local, the universal at the expense of the particular, the collective at the expense of the personal, and the monumental at the expense of the simple. Translated into economics, that means multinational corporations and outsourcing—regardless of rustbelts and unemployment and regardless of politics. It is no longer true that "all politics is local." Thus, America's political elites such as President Biden and his family, corporate titans such as Nike, billionaire sports owners, university administrations such as Harvard, and sports celebrities such as Lebron James have all in their turn held their noses and turned a blind eye to human rights and the plight of the Uighurs in making deals with repressive Chinese communists.

Translated into politics, it means talk of global governance and the New World Order—regardless of individual freedom and local customs. As Klaus Schwab argues, the pandemic was a key milestone because it showed three things: that no one was in charge of the world, that the way things were done before was not working, and the world must never go back to the old ways. Schwab's answer in all three cases is greater coordination and greater global control. His "new capitalism," creating a "safer, cheaper, greener world," requires increased global control. In his book *The Grand Reset*, he declares that "there cannot be lasting recovery without a global strategic framework of governance." Globalists by nature are citizens of the world rather than patriots of their homeland. "Never let a good crisis go to waste" is the globalist mantra that means using crises to expand the wider and wider applications of the rationality of the global expert and bureaucrat for the betterment of the rest of the world. "Politicians love chaos," John le Carré used to say. "It gives them authority." Pandemics, right- and left-wing politicians, and oligarchs all do the same.

Seen that way, globalism has become a worldview tinged with both staggering moneymaking potential and revolutionary utopian messianic dreams of universal brotherhood and harmony—as much so as the earlier revolutionary dreams of millenarianism, socialism, and communism. Globalism is a view of the world surveyed from the penthouse suite, the skyscraper boardroom, and the high-altitude perspective of a private jet. Not surprisingly, global talk has a natural bias toward the big Cs—*control* over *chaos* through the *centralized*, the *coordinated*, the *consolidated*, and the *collective*. Globalism is always rational, and global rationality means enhanced global authority encroaching on everyone everywhere—uniformity at the expense of diversity, and order without freedom at the expense of the local and the individual.

Globalism therefore naturally appeals to those such as billionaires Bill Gates and George Soros who are fired by revolutionary utopianism, and it favors the bookend of authoritarianism. In economics the natural outcome of globalism is a monopoly. (Think of the rise of Google, Amazon, and Facebook and their unprecedented control of our sources of information.) In politics the natural outcome of globalism is global governance and a new world order. (Think of the current fashion for state socialism, the emergence of one-party politics in ostensible democracies, the expansion of the ever-expanding European Union, and the global pretensions of "Belt and Road" superpower China.) The logic of globalism is autocracy, the logic of autocracy is technocracy, the logic of technocracy is bureaucracy, and the logic of bureaucracy is the replacement of genuine politics and representative government by administration and regulation. The result will be a cosmocracy, a beehive society, and an anthill state. Wake up, Members of Parliament and Congress, you may be lavishly remunerated by the financial seductions of corporate lobbyists, but you are in danger of becoming dupes and ciphers, the "useful idiots" of the globalist world that in effect is giving redundancy slips to you and all who believe in nation-states and representative government.

GLOBALIST ACTION, ANTIGLOBALIST REACTION

But if this globalist temptation is a natural child of globalization, so also are the antiglobalist fears it triggers. Hence the rise of populism and nationalism in reaction and even the resort to religion in a reactionary form that is the counterbalance to the revolutionary secularism of the globalist. The result is the antagonism between secularist globalism and religious nationalism, through which all patriots have become vulnerable to the charge of being nationalists. The fact is, however, that the elites who fulminate against nationalism recognize only the danger of the antiglobalist extreme and not the dangers of their own globalism. Their globalism is out to disempower all that stands in its way, including nation-states and local institutions of all kinds.

The truth is that what is completely invisible, or what looks messy and parochial from 30,000 feet, is what matters for ordinary people on the ground—including religion. Thus, viewed from the bottom rather than the top, which is the viewpoint of the populists: "We are all Uighurs now." Increasingly, the lives of ordinary people feel as if they are lived in society designed as a giant reeducation camp run by the oligarchs of the ruling class—the "best and brightest" experts and professionals of the globalist elite, with the help of countless academic studies, billions of cameras, and data-devouring mobile phones.

Think of the grandiose visions of the largest foundations and the wealthiest billionaires. Day by day they scientifically nudge us toward their goals, and they advise and supervise the state's steady encroachment on the authority of parents over the lives of their own children or cite the authority of "science" to justify the policies of the moment. ("Follow the science" means "Obey the scientist who has the power.") What was once freedom of speech and robust debate is re-branded by the elites as dissidence, what was once personal opinion is now disinformation, and too much of the politically incorrect dissidence and disinformation of ordinary people runs the risk of being outlawed as domestic terrorism.

Little wonder, the populists feel, it is time for the ruled to strike back against the rulers and the controlled to throw off the controllers. The globalist drive feels like a high-tech coup by the unelected and the megawealthy. By what standards of human justice could the billionaires double their fortunes during the pandemic while the rest of humanity suffered? If womb-to-tomb monitoring and surveillance are the price of safety, many people would prefer freedom with all its messiness and risks. With increasing hindsight, it is now clear that Donald Trump's most important, if ironic, contribution to America was this: in rousing the visceral disdain of the elites and the massed forces of disgust against him, he highlighted with unmistakable clarity the post-democratic, one-party technocratic elites that have emerged in America to replace American democracy with America's newly forming authoritarian oligarchy.

The combined force of globalization and globalism creates its own advanced modern caste system. Moneymakers have long been America's aristocracy. Successful globalists are now the titans of modernity's aristocracy, the Mandarin class who have risen by the merit of their own genius and thus are obviously superior and deserving. (Think of Jeff Bezos, Elon Musk, Bill Gates, George Soros, Michael Bloomberg, Mark Zuckerberg, and their peers and their plans for colonizing the world and then space.) All who are beneath them obviously "have less because they deserve less," and at the bottom of the system are Hillary Clinton's infamous "deplorables." They are the little people and the untouchable caste who, as Barack Obama put it, "cling to their God and their guns," and form what George W. Bush called the "foul stench" of American extremism.

Clearly, the deplorables are the Dalits of the modern world and their task is to serve the Brahmin caste. Their good fortune as peasants is to comply with the Mandarin experts and the elites who are our best and brightest and who therefore know what is best for us all. Contrary to utopian democrats, the voice of the people is never the voice of God, but it is no less dangerous to replace the divine right of kings and peoples with the quasi-divine right of the elite, the technocrat, the expert, and the oligarch.

The mark of true leadership is a leader's understanding of the people, belief in the people, and compassion for the people the leader is leading. But unsurprisingly, America's pretentious and unbridled meritocracy has created a gigantic gap between the elites and the people, the "better sort" and the rest of us, the ruling few and the toiling many. The global era is accelerating the opening of this gap to create the most monstrous inequality history has ever seen. Most obvious in terms of wealth, this inequality and the savage tensions it creates will prove a festering source of conflict in the world of the future—for all the progressive posturing of the elites. Such inequalities are rife with injustice, so of course they carry their own downward-spiraling momentum. The more control by the elites, the more resentment and protests from the populists; and the more unrest from the populists, the more drive to control by the elites.

Left unaddressed, a double desertion of the American experiment at both the top and the bottom is happening. In Arnold Toynbee's magisterial analysis of the decline of the West, *A Study in History*, he views the elites as the "once-creative minority" who no longer merit their power and privilege, but who will not give up either. The popularists are Toynbee's "internal proletariat" who are no longer Marx's industrial working class but those who are now alienated within a declining civilization. In America today, the swelling number of the cheated and forgotten proletarians are finding their voice, though an angry and resentful voice. And a ruling class that has lost all moral authority and almost all concerns but power will doubtless end in abusing power repeatedly. What could be more logical? If God is dead for all practical purposes, and promise-keeping is only provisional and a matter of "so long as it serves our interests," then increasingly the social bond relied on will be force.

Trace these various trends and their mounting tensions. Future conflicts are a possibility, though not the only one. Yet there is no need to slide toward authoritarianism from above or anarchy from below. Once the danger of this widening chasm is clearly understood (and from both sides) it underscores that there is one essential way to resist the pull of this

dangerous political and social whirlpool created by globalism. *The powerful thrust toward the global must be coun-
tered not by reaction, protest, and violence but by building an
equally powerful constructive counterthrust toward the local,
the personal, the private, and the deeply human and free.*

There is nothing, absolutely nothing, wrong with a proper
vision of the global. Both God and human nature will always
resist the pretensions of every Tower of Babel. The global has
been at the heart of the calling of Jews and Christians ever
since God's promise to Abraham that all the earth would be
blessed in him, reinforced by the Great Commission of Jesus.
Both faiths have a global vision in their DNA, but both also
have a balance between the global and the local, eternity and
the day to day ("Give us today our daily bread.") Today's globalists lack that balance. Need it be said that even our brave
new Prometheans have the same little bodies we all do? Even
if they build a score of megamansions and launch a fleet of
three hundred–foot superyachts, they can only live in them
one at a time and live one day at a time. Both the global and
the local must be thought through in terms of human dignity,
freedom, and justice. Is that even possible today? Is there a
vision of the personal and the human that is strong enough
to balance the rocket-fueled propulsion of the global? Is
there an offset strong enough to counter the reset? "Think
globally, act locally" is a noble ideal, but the maxim without
a method will never be more than a mirage.

Beware the strutting globalist who has no time for the
local, the billionaire who has no heart for injustice on the
other side of the world, the citizen of the world who forgets
what life is like in a parish, or the nerd who lives as if we all

live in our heads and not in our bodies. It is time and past time to explore the ancient Hebrew vision that was so strenuously seconded by George Washington—the vision of a home, a lively dining table, a healthy family, a strong neighborhood, and a good society that, whether small or large, forms a commonwealth of human dignity, liberty, and collective responsibility. The local is as important as the global, the private as much as the public, the particular as much as the universal. The parish matters as much as the world, and the inner-city apartment will always be the home to many more humans and to a more human way of life than the space station can ever be. Such is the deeply human picture of the personal and local freedom of living under our own vine and fig tree, and we dare not close our eyes to its challenges and its blessings.

PART TWO

FREEDOM'S
FOUNDATION
STONES

SET FREE TO BE FREE

DEFINING AND UNDERSTANDING FREEDOM

EVERYTHING SHOULD be made as simple as possible, but no simpler." Albert Einstein's famous maxim is as challenging for freedom as it is for science, and especially so for America and the West. No country and no civilization have ever made freedom so central to their ideals as America and the West, but none has ever tarnished freedom and made it so controversial as it has become today. The narrow path between impenetrable complication on one side and platitudinous cliché on the other has now been made perilous by philosophical, political, and theological controversies at every turn. Yet it is worth attempting. When it comes to freedom, the alternative is to give up on freedom and betray our humanity. To build and maintain families and communities that foster human worth, freedom, justice, peace, and stability may be harder than ever in the advanced modern world, but the task is also urgent and worthwhile.

What follows are brief reflections on seven essential and foundational aspects of freedom at the personal and local level. They are the simple essentials for life under our own vine and fig tree. Perfunctory lip service and an endless recirculation of truisms will never be enough to protect freedom. Some now say that Washington's vision of the vine and fig is redundant because it is covered by the long-established Catholic principle of *subsidiarity*. The goal of the principle of subsidiarity is laudable: to protect the authority of local powers from the overreach of higher and more central powers, and even the European Union has enshrined its support—in words. But as life in the global era shows, the new global will tend to outweigh the national, the national will outweigh the local, and bureaucracy will tend to over-power subsidiarity unless there is a robust, healthy, and un-deniable flourishing of freedom at the local level. Even the Latinized term *subsidiarity* is incomprehensible to many people. The truth is that the vision of living under our own vine and fig tree is as essential in the global era as it was in the days of George Washington and King Solomon earlier—only much harder to achieve today.

The brief statements in this chapter are short, though the chapter is long. Each of the seven points requires a fuller exposition to do justice to its importance. But even a brief statement can serve as a preliminary checklist and inspire further exploration and debate. Freedom always suffers from clichés as well as complacency, but freedom is a theme that requires and repays untiring thinking and debate. If the following account of freedom comes anywhere close to the truth, its principles and insights must be explored at greater depths that go far beyond this brief essay, and they should apply to local communities of all sorts, whether a family, a community, a neighborhood, or a country of many millions in a world of billions and billions.

Yet a warning is in order. We must set out on an exploration of freedom with humility and realism. The Hebrew exodus, recounted in the book by the same name, is the greatest and most influential liberation in all history. Exodus tells the story of the rescue of the utterly powerless from one of the most massive, powerful, and longest-lasting empires in all history. It is an event without parallel and the inspiration for countless later revolutions and liberation movements across the world. *But astonishingly, there is not a single mention of the word* freedom *in the main account in Exodus.* Unquestionably, the exodus and the book of Exodus that describes it are all about freedom—rescue, deliverance, liberation, freedom from slavery in an alien land, and freedom for a new way of life in Israel's land—yet there is no mention of the word.

Why? Among many possible reasons, the simplest is perhaps the Bible's realism. Freedom is always a means, never an end. But freedom is a means to an end that is so vital and so glorious that it easily becomes an end in itself, and freedom then undermines itself when magnified into an idol. Freedom is at the heart of the glory of being human. But freedom is also the greatest enemy of freedom, and the abuse of the power of freedom, above all the abuse of the power of some humans over other humans, is the greatest stain on the record of humanity. Like fire, which is both creative and destructive, freedom requires handling with care. Rape, murder, slavery, and genocide are the extremes of the abuse of the power of freedom, but the same abuse of freedom also operates daily and destructively in gossip, insult, and rumor-mongering. Talk of freedom calls for wise heads and humble hearts as well as rousing cheers.

There is no question that the picture of citizens living under their own vine and fig tree is a powerful vision of freedom. It provides the positive side to familiar negative slogans such as "Don't tread on me!" and "Not in my backyard, you don't." By themselves these slogans are important protests against any invasion of freedom, and they are rich in historical resonance. But they are purely negative, and without the positive side they can easily become selfish, reactionary, and even ugly. But the challenge is to throw sufficient light on the essence of freedom to make freedom fully understandable as well as practical and realistic. *What actually is freedom, and what does freedom require of those who would be free and stay free?* How may we achieve it and sustain it without falling for its temptations and distortions?

What becomes clear is that freedom is like a rare and beautiful jewel. It will never be fully appreciated from one perspective only. It must be turned around and around in our minds, examined in the light of different questions and admired from many different angles. No single angle allows its full brilliance to be seen, so the turning and the appreciation must keep going. Those who think they have arrived at the last word on freedom only show that they have stopped short. There is always more to be considered, more to be admired, and more to be learned. A brief book like this is no more than a modest attempt at the task, yet I hope that it will inspire fresh thinking about freedom that will serve the interests and challenges of our extraordinary moment in history.

There is no question that the Bible's and Washington's vision of freedom flows from its source, faith in God. In today's more diverse and secular society, many people will not share this viewpoint, but that is no excuse for the prejudice that dismisses it without thinking. Disagreements should be appreciative, not dismissive, and the challenge for those who differ is always to do better. The final authority for freedom in the Bible's view, unlike, say, that of secularists and those who follow the French Enlightenment, is faith in God rather than reliance on reason alone, nature alone, or history alone.

Some will claim that to argue from this foundation is either arbitrary or irrational, but it is as fully justifiable by reason as any of the other foundations for freedom. It is arguably more so. Reason cannot justify itself by itself, and reason is best justified within the bounds of revelation. This approach is also rational in the sense that the way faith makes freedom possible can easily be set out with solid reasons.

Needless to say, too, those who ground their freedom elsewhere are welcome to set out their case as they wish to. As ever, contrast will be the mother of clarity and time will be the test. My claim is simply that faith in God provides a foundation for freedom and for free societies that is rational, solid, and deserves fair consideration. Indeed, no other social and political vision or model comes close. But of course, exploring and weighing such claims and putting them to the test in real life is a central task of our time. What follows are brief reflections on the essential foundation stones or defining features of human freedom and free societies from the perspective of the Bible or the Jewish and Christian viewpoint.

Together, these seven defining features of freedom present an offer and mount a challenge; they form nothing less than the foundational forces for freedom that make for human flourishing, and therefore they raise several questions: Who will use this discussion of the foundation stones to assess contemporary views of freedom? Who will dare to apply them where there are gaping deficiencies over freedom in, say, American politics or schooling? And for those who still disagree with these principles, where are your better alternatives? In sum, these seven foundational features carry a straightforward warning: *freedom is appealing because it lies at the heart of a life worthy of life, but freedom is challenging because freedom pursued by any who ignore its character and dynamics becomes a slipway to disillusion, dissatisfaction, and slavery.* There are many more who cry freedom and pursue freedom than find freedom in a fulfilling and lasting form. What then is freedom, and what does freedom require of those who would be free?

Freedom, at its heart, is simply *the ability to make genuine choices, to live with the consequences of our choices, and so to be truly able to be ourselves.* Like any subject, freedom must begin with a clear definition and an understanding of what it means and what it is we are talking about and striving for. At the heart of this definition and understanding of freedom are three truths that, in their turn, are indispensable to our view of freedom and to our becoming free as human beings. This basic notion sounds simple and rather obvious, and it would be widely shared by many people, though no one should be deceived by the apparent consensus. Far-reaching differences rise at once in terms of how the definition itself is to be understood, and some of the disagreements will lead in very different directions. Let's begin our turning of the diamond of freedom by looking at the essential elements that make up the heart and soul of freedom.

TO BE FREE IS TO BE SET FREE TO BE WHO WE ARE

Freedom is so much the essence of humanity that to eliminate freedom is an act of freedom that eliminates ourselves. But what is freedom? *The heart of human freedom is the capacity for genuine choice and thus the ability to be who we are and so to be ourselves, to think for ourselves, to speak for ourselves, and to choose and act in line with who we are and what we choose.* The goal of freedom is nothing less than the full flourishing of human persons who become free to be the people they were born on earth to be and thus to live a life worthy of life. The three basic political rights—freedom of religion and conscience, freedom of speech, and freedom of assembly or association—are simply the rights designed to protect this understanding of human freedom. At a deeper level still, the Jewish and Christian faiths have freedom at their core. Coming together from many angles, their central truths are nothing less than faiths for freedom.

Notice that stated this way freedom sounds simple. "Be who you are!" But of course, neither *the capacity for choice* nor *being who we are* are as simple as they sound. First, it is important to see that freedom is a means, an ability, and a capacity. Freedom is not in itself an end, though the goal of becoming free to be able to exercise and enjoy that means can become an important end—an addict getting off drugs for example or a prisoner getting out of jail to lead a new life. Freedom is essentially a means and an ability—to be who we are—and it therefore assumes and requires answers to other underlying questions, such as Who are we as human beings? What is our end, our purpose, and our direction in life? Are we free from the very start of life, at birth? And what sort of factors or forces might stop us from being free to be who we are so that we need to be set free to be free?

The complications multiply further when we take account of the subjective dimension of freedom. Freedom has to be internal as well as external. People may be as externally and politically free as any people have ever been, but they will only feel free if they have inner freedom to match their outer freedom, and thus a healthy balance between the sum total of their desires and the sum total of their means. Means are much more than money, of course, but money makes the point simply. One hundred dollars will not go far in buying someone the home of their dreams or a superyacht, so those who have inadequate means or inordinate desires will never know the inner freedom of contentment.

Yet the very *raison d'être* of a consumer society is designed to be the sworn enemy of contentment and therefore of full inner freedom. *Enough* will never be enough, and it is not meant to be. How much is enough is always John D. Rock-efeller's "Just a little bit more." Such a stoking of insatiable desire is the heart of consumerism. Consumerism depends on mimesis or desiring what others desire, which of course is the driving appeal of advertising. Freedom in a consumer society will therefore appear to many people as a mirage—unless some are able to increase their means, others are able to decrease their desires, and enough people know how to do both. The Rolling Stones' famous cry "Can't get no satisfaction" is at once the nightmare of the consumer and the shining dream of the advertiser.

All of which, in turn, asks, What is the truth of the meaning of the answers to these questions, including the question, Do our desires match our means, and are our desires good and reasonable? In short, freedom sounds simple, but it is far from simple. Full answers to the questions of freedom must delve into the realm of the philosophical and the spiritual as well as the political and the economic. Almost everyone can agree on the opening statement about freedom, but as soon as we raise the later questions, people will find themselves going in a score of different directions, according to their view of the world and their philosophy of life.

If freedom is essentially a means and not an end, it depends crucially on the ends it is the means to. Certain important consequences follow. First, freedom assumes and requires truth, the understanding of *the reality of reality*. Unless we know the truth of the meaning of life and thus of our nature and our end as human beings, we would neither know who we are nor how we are to think, speak, and choose and act freely as ourselves. This means we will have to consider different claims in assessing what is true, remain humble in asserting our claims about what we believe to be true, and (if only for the sake of freedom) be persuasive rather than coercive in our dealings with those who differ from us. But one conclusion is indisputable at the very outset. Today's claims about the undecidability of truth in our post-truth world represent a flat-out contradiction of freedom and form an impassable quicksand that bogs down any hope of achieving freedom. America, take note. No nation that subscribes to the postmodern view of truth can expect its freedom to be strong or to last. Jesus states the alternative more realistically: "You will know the truth, and the truth will make you free" (John 8:32). Without truth, there can be no liberty and no liberation.

Second, freedom has to be both negative and positive. It always has two parts. The great Jewish philosopher Isaiah Berlin was famous for his insistence that freedom always has two aspects. Both have to be borne in mind, and neither is complete without the other. First, to be free, we must have negative freedom. We must be *free from*, free from anyone and anything that constrains us wrongly in the light of the truth of who we are and who we are meant to be. The menace to our freedom may come from internal problems, such as the vices of pride, envy, anger, sloth, avarice, gluttony, and lust (once known as the seven deadly sins), or it may come from an external problem, such as a schoolyard bully, an abusive parent, addiction to alcohol or drugs, a political tyrant, or a false ideology.

For Christians in particular this insistence on negative freedom as well as positive freedom reinforces a consideration that underlies the entire understanding of freedom. Humans are created to be free, called to be free, capable of becoming free, *but to be free, we need to be set free*. Can any of us look at our own lives and history and seriously hold the view that humans are naturally, completely, and constantly good, and there is nothing wrong with humanity? Hardly. Only a simpleton or a narcissist could look at humanity and think that. Everyone who loves freedom knows that there is a chronic problem with humanity and certainly with freedom. Freedom repeatedly goes wrong—misused and abused. Indeed, all abuse, whether verbal abuse in insults or physical abuse in rape or murder, is an abuse of freedom. The paradox of freedom is that the greatest enemy of freedom is freedom. This means that we must investigate what it is that bedevils our hearts, clouds our minds, biases our choices, and ruins our best intentions by twisting freedom into a travesty of freedom that at its worst leads to our denying freedom either by abusing others or by addicting ourselves.

To be free, we need to be set free, yet this *freedom from* is only the start. We must also have positive freedom. We must be *free for, free to be* all we are supposed to be in light of the truth of who we are. Set free, we must live free. Liberation from any captivity is glorious, whether from a vice, prison, drugs, alcohol, a tyrannical boss, a political despot, or plain old selfishness, but liberation is only *freedom from* and the first step in the story.

Liberty is more than liberation, and full freedom is not so much a moment as a way of life. Lopsided stress on negative freedom is a damning weakness of many contemporary views of freedom, such as libertarianism ("Don't tread on me," again). Such negative freedom by itself will only ever be reactionary. Without positive freedom, it can never be constructive. This means that the two sides of freedom must never be separated. As philosopher and ethicist Leon Kass writes, "Getting human beings out of slavery is easy; getting slavishness—and tyranny—out of human beings is hard." Or as the rabbis say about the exodus from Egypt, "It took God one day to get the Jews out of Egypt, but it took God forty years and more to get Egypt out of the Jews."

Third, freedom is freedom, and it carries its own intrinsic requirements. *Freedom is not the permission to do what we like, but the power to do what we ought.* That brief sentence contains one of the great dividing lines in understanding freedom. It highlights the most common oversight in understanding freedom—the fact that freedom has requirements, such as truth, character, and a way of life. It also highlights the most seductive of the many distortions of freedom, which is usually stated with a nuanced addition: "Choose whatever you like, and do whatever you choose, *so long as you do no harm*." The simplicity in that maxim is beguiling but deceptive. There are two principles in the sentence—the *choice principle* and the *harm principle*. Neither is as straightforward as it sounds, and they can easily be set against each other until they rule each other out.

From one side, the harm principle can be used to undermine freedom by restricting it. Anyone who disagrees with someone else's freedom has only to claim that they or society itself are harmed by it, and the freedom must be cut down at once. Think of the culturally trained hypersensitivities to microaggression, dissing, and the need for "safe places." Whatever they disagree with, they declare they are harmed by. Cry "harm," and the whole tumbril machinery of the speech codes, the cancel culture, and the high-tech censors will be fired into action, and freedom of speech and expression will be shut down. That is how "liberal," "democratic," and "progressive" people become illiberal, authoritarian, and regressive. It is how colleges and corporations such as Google and Facebook have come to censor and cancel freedoms with all the heavy-handedness of the Soviets and the Maoists while still professing that they are defending liberalism and fighting for democracy.

From the other side, the choice principle does the opposite. It undermines freedom by inflating it impossibly. Anything you wish to do and choose to do yourself is freedom, made "authentic" by the imprimatur of your personal choice—even if, for example, it means that you choose drink, drugs, or sex to the point of obsession and addiction and the complete loss of freedom. That is the folly through which the "land of the free" has come to have more addictions and recovery groups than any country in the world. Freedom has run riot. Freedom has gone to seed.

Too many Americans emphasize the choice principle, forget the harm principle, and end up harming themselves. Currently, the vanguard of America's define-yourself, flout-all-categories-and-boundaries assertion of freedom is the transgender movement. Liberation means overcoming the givens of sex and bodies, and the long-term results will be another tragic variation on the Rolling Stones' lament, "Can't get no satisfaction." But transgenderism is not the ultimate revolt. It will soon be overtaken by transhumanism. The ultimate cure for dysphoria will not be freedom for females trapped in a male body or for males trapped in a female body, but techno-freedom and pseudo-immortality for humans trapped in bodies of any kind—a grand recycling of ancient Gnosticism in a high-tech guise and the prelude to restlessness and discontent without end.

The revolutionary liberationism of the radical left is in breathless pursuit of a phantom—the utopian fantasy of a fully free society liberated from beliefs, bodies, boundaries, binaries, and all that bottles up our instincts. That is where the second addition enters the discussion. Restrictions born of the fear of harm, they say, cause even greater harm than the purported misuse of freedom. Thus, whereas many people argue that internet pornography, rap music, and video games reinforce violence and the abuse of women, the radicals argue that these are artistic expressions, and they reduce violence by providing a safety valve to blow off the aggression. The greater danger, they argue, lies in denying our instincts and bottling up our desires—the "return of the repressed" or "what you ban, you bring on." The solution they propose is to "decriminalize everything," from drugs to prostitution. Then there will be no foothold for organized crime, and what is no longer considered wrong requires no judging, labeling, or policing—and everyone can be happy, free, and fulfilled on their own terms.

Are such liberationists correct? Only the psychological and social harvest that will ripen on some day after tomorrow will settle the argument conclusively, but it is not hard to see how confusion, anxiety, brokenness, loneliness, and despair will reach epidemic proportions—when the triumph of the therapeutic will be the flip side of the human catastrophe that needs to be healed.

In the meantime the double political strategy of the radicals is clear: cry freedom and provide every incentive to make absolute freedom possible and remove every moral and legal barrier that makes absolute freedom impossible. The certainty, in the end, will be more than a mental health problem. It will be a moral, social, and civilizational disaster. Human freedom is linked essentially to truth and reality, so there are actions and ways of life that appear to be free but do not align with reality and therefore lead to the opposite of freedom—obsessions, addictions, dissatisfaction, disease, and death.

To live well, love well, choose wisely, and do good, freedom requires truth, freedom requires character, and freedom requires a way of life that is aligned with freedom. Just as we must eat well and exercise well to be healthy, so we must live well to be free. Unfortunately, the Hebrew word *torah* has become encrusted with negative and legalistic connotations in English. Translated as "law," it is viewed solely as legislation and treated as a series of regulations passed into law to restrict our freedom. Its real meaning is the opposite. *Torah* is "instruction" or "teaching"—God's loving instructions for life, his coaching us on how to live well together.

There is a striking consensus among most of the religions of the world as well as the majority of classical thinkers that freedom is linked to virtue and that unbridled passions are the enemy of freedom as they are of virtue. Only in the modern world, and especially in America, do we find the foolish notion that the passions may be indulged in pursuit of the "real you" and the "real me," regardless of truth, regardless of right and wrong, and regardless of the reality of our bodies. Uncomfortable though it is to us as modern people, the "10,000 hours principle" applies to freedom as much as to piano playing, pole vaulting, and public speaking. Freedom is both an art and a moral achievement, and eternal discipline is as much the price of liberty as eternal vigilance.

TO BE FREE IS TO BE FREE AND RESPONSIBLE

At the heart of freedom is responsibility. A free human being is a responsible human being, and the greatest test of freedom is the way a free person and a free people handle the responsibilities of freedom. The very act of thinking and saying "I" or "we" is an expression of agency, freedom, and responsibility. There is no one who does not think or say "I" at some point in life, however limited the sphere in which we may say it and act on it. To be ourselves is to think as *I*, speak as *I*, and act as *I*. To be free is therefore to think freely, speak freely, and act freely as ourselves, including the ability to be able to choose freely and respond as we choose, even in the face of massive censorship and coercion. Under the most extreme circumstances, such as torture, we still always have one final freedom: our ability to make second-order evaluations—in other words, to stand back and choose the attitude with which we respond to the vilest abuse and humiliation we may face. That agency and that freedom, as Viktor Frankl and other World War II death-camp inmates recorded after their liberation, was a silver lining in the otherwise unrelieved horror of the Holocaust.

The responsibility of human significance and freedom is of course qualified in several ways, above all for Jews and Christians by the mystery of God's sovereignty and therefore of his providence overarching history and giving it purpose. Abraham Lincoln and countless others have pondered this truth, in Lincoln's case with deep fruitfulness but with disastrous consequences in the thinking of many others. But while God's providence frames human responsibility, it does not rule it out. Whether our room for choice is wide or narrow, freedom always means choosing between choices, acting on the choices we have chosen, and shouldering the consequences for the choices we have made. If each of us, saying "I" at least in our inner selves, had not chosen as we did, each choice could have been otherwise, and each choice only happened as it did because we chose it. Genuine freedom therefore means the agency of shouldering responsibility for the specific choices we did make, and for whatever we have willed and chosen to say, to do, and to bring into being. No child, no slave, and no robot is free and responsible in the way we adult humans are.

The responsibility of freedom stands squarely between two extremes: a slavish attitude at one end and a spoiled attitude at the other. The slave-minded attitude, whether in real chattel slavery or in emotional and psychological slavery, is allowed next to no responsibility because slavery is a boot camp in enforced dependency under the control of others. The spoiled attitude is irresponsible rather than nonresponsible because a spoiled person chooses to assert their rights with a blithe unconcern for their responsibilities—to the point where they become dependent on others unwittingly. (This is the rich-kids' equivalent of the welfare dependency of the poor when an indulgent parent or family trust fund replaces the government handout.) In strong contrast to both these extremes, a free person and a free people are those who, as agents, choose freely and are answerable for themselves, for their actions, and for the consequences of their actions.

Responsibility means, for example, that the person who makes a promise and gives their word becomes a debtor to other people, and the person (or people) the promise is made to become the creditor. The promise made may be minor and only implicit ("See you for lunch tomorrow") or it may be major and highly explicit (such as the marriage covenant "till death do us part"). But such is the responsibility of the promise-maker that the future is mortgaged until the promise is kept. Only then, when the person carries out what they have willed, is the debt discharged. Responsibility is therefore integral to agency and freedom, and it is through responsibility that promises are made and kept, trust is built, and the bonds and ties of marriage, community, and nationhood are kept healthy and strong.

In Robert Bolt's play and later film *A Man for All Seasons*, Sir Thomas More refuses to save his life by weaseling over an oath he has to swear to King Henry VIII. His clever lawyer daughter Margaret advises him to "say the words of the oath and in your heart think otherwise." But that equivocation is something her father cannot and will not do, even if his refusal means signing his own death warrant. "When a man takes an oath, Meg, he's holding his own self in his own hands. And if he opens his fingers then—he needn't hope to find himself again. Some men aren't capable of this, but I'd be loath to think your father one of them."

This responsibility of freedom is challenging, consequential, and a matter of realism rather than idealism. Freedom does not mean that because we are free, we can choose to be responsible if we wish to be—as if responsibility were a bonus activity for the superachieving virtuous. Responsibility, rather, is the essence of freedom. *Freedom means that precisely because we are free we are responsible for better or worse and whether we like it or not. Responsibility means too that because we are free and responsible, we would cease to be fully free and to be ourselves if we fail to be responsible.* When we exercise our will to make our own choices and make our promises to the future, we are responsible for the consequences that always follow. Some results will be intended and some unintended and unforeseeable, but freedom means that free people shoulder the responsibility for the results as part and parcel of what it means for them to be free, to have made the promise, and to be committed to keeping the promise that has been made. Our word is our bond until we have fulfilled what we said—political candidates included.

In the advanced modern world, the spoiled extreme is more common than the slavish extreme. Our age is obsessed with entitlement and rights rather than responsibility. Our age is also the golden age of exoneration: we are well-schooled in the art of passing the buck and blaming someone else. And now our age has the Gyges ring of invisibility through travel and the internet so that in more and more of life we are anonymous and unaccountable. In such a world the responsibility and the duty at the heart of freedom get short shrift—which is yet another reason why our freedom is decaying, why our social bonds are unraveling, and why there is so little honor and so few resignations in America after major public scandals—unlike Europe.

(Where there is no responsibility and no honor, one can always brazen things out.)

Yet true freedom and responsibility are inseparable. They are at the very heart of growing up into adult life and into the full membership of a family, a community, or a nation. Where there is no desire to lead a responsible life, as with an endlessly delayed adolescence, or where there is no room to do so, as in societies with excessive authoritarian control, there is no freedom. Free societies are responsible societies, with citizens who stand ready to answer for their commitments at every level. They know how to say "we" as well as "I." They are ready, willing, and able to assume the personal and public responsibility that both self-government and citizenship require.

RESPONSIBILITY MEANS PROTEST

Think for a moment and you can see how the responsibility of freedom rings a bell in many different areas. The Hebrew for responsibility, *'ahrayut*, comes from the word for "other," *'aher*. Responsibility is simply the act of responding appropriately to the *other* of people, situations, and moments outside ourselves. Such responding begins supremely with faith itself, for faith is our response to God's call and his reaching out to us. Indeed, for both Jews and Christians, God is the supreme Other, and responding to God's call to himself is the first step in a life of responsibility.

For those who come to know him, there is no greater Other in our lives than God, our Creator and the final source of life and reality itself. The heart of faith is the response that encounters God and says "Here I am" in answer to God's searching question to each of us and to all humanity, "Where are you?" This responsibility is what makes Abraham the father of the faithful. God calls and he responds, and from then on Abraham lived before one audience, the audience of One. Indeed, unlike many who came before him, Abraham was history's first responder, and his response to God's call was the precedent and pattern of his life of responsibility in other areas—his personal responsibility for his nephew Lot, his moral responsibility for the captives carried off by the marauding invaders, and his collective responsibility for the people of Sodom threatened with God's judgment.

At a very different level, though connected, freedom's responsibility is at the heart of protest against the *wrong other* of injustice in the world. In the Bible's view, sin, evil, wrong, injustice, and abuse are all the result of the misuse and abuse of freedom, and central to them all is a refusal to take responsibility. (Adam's "The woman whom You gave to be with me . . ." is a refusal of personal responsibility, Cain's "Am I my brother's keeper?" is a refusal of moral responsibility, and the builders of the Tower of Babel represent a refusal of existential responsibility.) Evil and wrongs create an *other* in the world or conditions in society that are *entirely wrong and should have been otherwise.*

Things have gone awry. They were never meant to be this way. The right and natural response to the wrongness of evil should be the responsibility of outraged justice in protest. The situation is abuse that cries out for a response, and the right response is a vigorous moral protest against what is morally wrong, leading to resolute practical action to do what is needed to put it right.

The Jewish and Christian faiths are protest faiths. Jews and Christians are protesters. They never simply adjust to the world or resign themselves to life, because the world as it stands is a world gone wrong. It is not what it should have been, and it is not what it should be and will be. This means that the People of the Book do not accept the world as it is, and while truly conservative, they are never purely conservative. The world has gone wrong, so there are wrongs to put right and things that are right, just, true, good, and beautiful to be restored or brought into existence. Trust in the God of the Bible is automatically a protest against the world as it is in the light of the world, which it should be and one day will be again.

The first such protest in history is Abraham's challenge to God over Sodom, which seems to be prompted by God himself. It is the first example of what the Jews call an "argument on behalf of heaven" in which it is legitimate to argue even with God if arguing on behalf of his creation. When God tells Noah of the judgment to come in the flood, Noah remains silent, but when God tells Abraham of the judgment to fall on Sodom and Gomorrah, Abraham protests. "Will You indeed sweep away the righteous with the wicked? . . . Shall not the Judge of all the earth deal justly?" (Genesis 18:23, 25). Abraham, the "father of the faithful," is the pioneer of protest.

No lawgiver is above the law, even if the lawgiver is God himself. Where the other before us is potentially wrong, we must raise questions. Where the other is a status quo that is wrong, we must challenge it. Where the other is evil, we must protest and resist. Whether the protest is allowed as a political right will depend on the country and the political system people are living in. Such protest will be easier in some countries than in others—in an English-speaking democracy, for example, rather than in authoritarian Russia or communist China. But the moral point lies deeper. For human beings in every country and through all time, protest against wrong and injustice is a moral and a human situation we must take responsibility for.

There is never a single moment in life when we humans do not have some collective responsibility for our fellow humans simply because of solidarity with our common humanity and our membership of some specific human community. As John Donne wrote with immortal brilliance in his *Devotions upon Emergent Occasions*, "No man is an island entire of itself." Even for the smallest and weakest person in the direst situation there at least can be the protest of prayer that cries out to God for justice. In contrast, the silence of consent that fails to protest evil is both faithless toward God and humanity. A refusal to protest and a refusal to take any responsibility at all is especially outrageous in covenantal and constitutional societies where the reciprocal responsibility of all for all is foundational to the political order (the Bible's "You shall love your neighbor as yourself"; the Three Musketeers' "All for one and one for all"; the US Constitution's "We the people . . ."). "Every Jew is responsible for every Jew," and by the same covenantal logic "Every American is responsible for every American," and by the same token of collective solidarity "Every human is responsible for every human."

RESPONSIBILITY MEANS LEADERSHIP

At a different level again, responsibility is the very heart and soul of leadership. Leaders such as presidents, CEOs, and captains may be at the head of nations, corporations, and teams. They may be at the front of movements or campaigns. But in the biblical view being at the top or in the front is not what matters in leadership, and it is not what makes leaders real leaders. Far deeper than that, *the essence of leadership is taking responsibility—a person taking responsibility for the other—for people, for a situation, or for a moment that is right in front of them.* We are each called to be leaders in this sense: to take responsibility in our own circles to do what we can do in response to what we see needs to be done—responsibility for a person, for a community, for a nation, and for seizing an opportunity or resolving a crisis.

It is a major mistake to think of leadership as only at the top of society or an organization. The fact is, there are people in authority and in formal positions of power who demonstrate little leadership, and there are people who have no official authority or formal positions yet who are powerful leaders and exert enormous influence. The influence of the Hebrew prophets, for example, has done far more to combat injustice than all the Hebrew kings combined. The same is true of Frederick Douglass, Booker T. Washington, Harriet Tubman, Rosa Parks, and Martin Luther King Jr. They had neither formal authority nor powerful positions, yet their influence for freedom and justice has outstripped the work of almost all the American presidents and Supreme Court justices. This take-responsibility character of leadership is the reason why a free society flourishes when there is leadership in every sphere and at every level, not only at the top.

In sum, freedom at its heart means responsibility. Free people are responsible people. True freedom means that free people make choices that are consequential, and whatever the unforeseen consequences or unexpected aftermaths, there is no shrugging off the fact that those who made the choices acted freely and therefore stand responsible for the outcome of their choices.

TO BE FREE REQUIRES RESPECT FOR THE EQUAL FREEDOM OF OTHERS

No man is an island, and neither are we Robinson Crusoe castaways living in the cosmos all by ourselves. We are all part of the greater continent of humanity, which raises the social and political challenge of freedom. Any freedom or right that we claim for ourselves by virtue of our humanity must at once be accorded equally to all others who are human too. Freedom therefore includes not only the first two elements, our ability to choose and our responsibility for our choices, but a third and even more difficult element: *mutual respect for the equal freedom and responsibility of others.*

The difficulty with this respect for the mutuality of freedom is often masked by the eloquence of the declarations guarding it—"A right for one is a right for another and a responsibility for both," "Injustice anywhere is injustice everywhere," and so on. What sounds eloquent is made to sound easy, and we nod approvingly. But the immensity of the practical challenge should also be obvious. My right to assert my freedom may at some point pose a threat to your right to assert your freedom, just as yours may pose a threat to mine. Thus, our respect for each other's freedom will almost certainly mean some curtailing of our freedom in some way. The paradox is plain. Freedom means self-expression, but it may also mean self-restraint, self-limitation, and even self-sacrifice, which is self-limitation with a price tag. In other words, each person's space to be free poses a potential threat to the space others need to be free, at least in principle. The more people there are in the equation or in the overall space, the more challenging the task of maximizing freedom for the benefit of everyone equally.

The challenge is simple to see. The more crowded the space, such as a dance floor, the harder it is to avoid stepping on someone else's toes, and so it is with freedom. For a hundred people in a community to respect the freedom of the other ninety-nine fellow members might be simple. For a million people the challenge would be harder, and for several hundred million or a billion it would be more difficult still. Some people even argue that the size of a community or nation puts an inevitable limit on freedom. Democracy, they say, may be workable in a city-state such as Athens, but it is impossible in a populous country such as China. (There were around three million Americans at the time of the revolution in 1776. Today there are more than three hundred million.) To be sure, Daniel Defoe's Robinson Crusoe enjoyed more freedom than we do, but only because for most of his twenty-eight years as a castaway he was completely alone until he met Friday. He was free to do whatever he liked because there was no one else in his world to consider.

The challenge of the mutuality of freedom within a community cuts two ways. Each person reaches out in freedom in both words and deeds as the expression of their common rights as humans, and each person's right returns to them as a potential threat from the equal rights of others. This demanding challenge of the mutuality of freedom requires two responses: first, an initial commitment from each person to consider self-restraint at some point, to respect the freedom of others; second, an ongoing commitment to political negotiation to work out how to maximize freedom for all and for the common good. As the Bible sees it, self-restraint is at the heart of freedom in creation. To create humans free, God limits himself. *He will not enter the human heart unless invited.* Self-restraint is equally at the heart of human community. If each of us is to respect the freedom of the other person, we must each respect the point at which we have no right to enter or interfere *unless the other person freely chooses to let us in.*

The central locus of freedom is the heart, and respect for freedom begins with respect for the inner forum of freedom of conscience. The search is always on for the best political model of freedom for all, a vision that protects foundational freedoms for everyone while allowing for the negotiation of inevitable disagreements that come from living together with our deepest differences. As populations grow and societies change, this search must be ongoing, and no generation is likely to have the final answer.

7

UNDERSTOOD UPWARD

HUMAN FREEDOM GROUNDED IN GOD

FOR HUMANS TO talk of freedom is quintessentially human, natural, and irrepressible, but is freedom real, and is it grounded? Are we human beings truly free? Freedom talk rings hollow unless we know that our freedom is solidly founded and truly authorized. That simple insistence is a sticking point for many people's view of freedom today. There are many more claims about freedom and protests on behalf of freedom than there are solid foundations for the claims and protests. Freedom is a common cry in the modern world. From the English Revolution (1642) to the American (1776), the French (1789), the Russian (1917), the Chinese (1949), and the myriad attempted revolutions, the chorus of human cries for freedom has risen to an unprecedented crescendo in the modern world. Yet most of those crying out have no more of a solid basis for their aspirations than Babylonian slaves, Chinese peasants, and medieval serfs could muster in their time. Even more oddly, much of the loudest clamor for human rights today is from those who are unable to justify the basis of the rights they clamor for.

The truth is that much modern thinking flatly denies that we humans are free. So, is there a sure and solid foundation for our human desire for freedom? Are we in fact as free as we think we are? For those who wish to live freely under their own vine and fig tree, this is an unavoidable question.

IN OUR STARS OR IN OUR GENES

There is no doubt about two things. First, freedom by its very nature will always be partly a mystery. If it could be described and analyzed with complete accuracy, it could be calculated and predicted with precision—which would be the end of freedom. Second, our human sense of freedom begins with our insider knowledge—our awareness of ourselves. We think, we feel, and we believe in our hearts that we are free and that we make genuine choices, so we must be free, or so we imagine. Think of the many choices we consciously make every single day. Imagine what experiences like falling in love would be if we knew conclusively that our love was no more than a matter of chemistry or the arrival of a full moon. But is it a cop-out to call freedom a mystery, and is such insider knowledge all there is to freedom? It certainly counts as evidence for something, but is that enough?

As a counterweight to the insider knowledge of feeling that we are free, we have to remember that most humans throughout history have been reminded by most of their rulers, philosophers, and religious leaders that they should do what they were told because they were not free. The philosopher Spinoza argued in his *Epistle* 58 that if a stone thrown through the air was given consciousness, it would believe it was free. For the Babylonians with their sophisticated astrology, life was determined by the stars. For the Hindus and Buddhists, our lives are determined by our *karma* ("Just as a calf will find its mother among a thousand cows, so your sins will find you out among a thousand generations"). For the Greeks, for all their celebration of the glory of humanity, life was determined by *moira* (fate) or by *anankē* (necessity). In Sophocles' *Oedipus Rex*, for example, both Oedipus and his father, Laius, do everything they can to ensure that the oracle at Delphi is not fulfilled—only to find that those very efforts make doubly sure that the oracle is proved true and all the more tragically so because of their resolute efforts to prevent it. What was considered freedom was really fate, and under such circumstances human life is a tragedy.

Many people today presume that as modern people we are different and that freedom is one of the issues that sets us over against the ancients and the traditional world. We believe in freedom, and we have good reasons for doing so, people think. Modernity, after all, is about choice. Fatalism may have been part and parcel of the ancient world, but freedom is surely at the heart of modernity. Choice and choices of all kinds are the warp and woof of all we do, from grand global decisions about politics and economics to couples falling in love, families furnishing a home, students applying to colleges, and all of us sitting in front of the computers every day.

Indeed, the right to choose is considered almost sacred today. People hold choice to be so important that by itself it is supposed to confer validity on what is chosen regardless of any other factors—in the debate over abortion, for example, the "right to choose" is said to trump all other considerations, moral or otherwise. Even the notion of authenticity has been narrowed down to a matter of whether people have chosen or consented to something themselves. Choice today is hallowed as sacred. Choice confers validity, and choice confirms dignity. Who then can doubt that we moderns are free?

Yet surprisingly, perhaps, this widespread assumption about modernity and freedom is quite wrong. Many of the most distinguished contemporary thinkers insist that we are not free. They believe in determinism as strongly, if not more strongly, as the ancients, though for a different reason. The irony is plain. Modern people started to prize freedom and search for freedom at the very moment when their leading thinkers were denying its existence. Listen to the chorus of modern secularist thinkers, from Karl Marx, Sigmund Freud, Bertrand Russell, J. B. Watson, B. F. Skinner, and Richard Dawkins to Sam Harris and Yuval Harari, and the refrain is the same. If only we knew all the forces determining our choices as they do (genetic, chemical, psychological, social and economic, and so on), we would see that human freedom is an illusion or a fiction. If we understood the complete chain of cause and effect, we would realize that nothing can be otherwise than it is. Human life, they insist, is a matter of chance and necessity. The front cover of philosopher Sam Harris's *Free Will* says it all. Freedom is a fiction, and what we take to be freedom is no more than a puppet dangling on the end of strings.

The reason is that atheists and secularists rely solely on naturalistic science or on the scientific method alone, so they can never discover freedom or deliver any verdict on whether there is such a thing as freedom. Their method rules out freedom by definition. Bertrand Russell stated the issue baldly in his book *Religion and Science*: "What science cannot discover, man cannot know." That is the coldblooded verdict of scientism or of naturalistic science taken as the be-all and end-all of human knowledge. It pronounces a death sentence on freedom. What the rest of us still call freedom is only "so-called freedom" or a "freedom of the gaps"—what we have not yet been able to explain causally but sooner or later we will. Naturalistic science militates against freedom by its very nature. Thus, for many atheists, freedom is no longer either possible or desirable. Freedom is no longer possible because if everything is caused, freedom is ruled out completely, and freedom is no longer desirable because it introduces an element of unpredictability into the scientist's quest for a Theory of Everything that is able to map all possible causes and explain the universe itself.

Our concern here is freedom itself, but there is no question that the full consequences of the denial of freedom would be widespread and practical in many areas. Many years ago Joseph Wood Krutch warned about the totalitarian implications of determinism in his book *The Measure of Man*. If the "science of man" is reduced to the "science of what humans would be if they were not human but machines," the result would play into the hands of the authoritarians. Self-government would be impossible for "subhumans." Those forced to acknowledge that they were completely determined from the inside and below would sooner or later find themselves determined and controlled from the outside and above.

Fortunately, there is an immense difference between science and scientism. It is no disparagement of the true importance of science or of the immense fruitfulness of the scientific method to acknowledge that, by definition, the very method cannot presume to discover freedom—there is more to reality than the scientific method can discover. The genius of the scientific method as a tool of discovery stands at the center of the enterprise of science itself. But important though science is, and fruitful though the scientific method has been, it is not the sole arbiter of truth and reality. Russell's dictum is simply wrong and preposterous. Love and freedom are only two of the highest human ideals that lie beyond the proof and disproof of the scientific method. The reason is that the method proceeds through its analysis of cause and effect. It works backward from a certain effect to what must have caused it, so of course it rules out freedom by definition. Human freedom works forward. By definition, freedom is undiscoverable in terms of cause and effect. It is rooted in the heart and mind, the will and the desire of the chooser.

LIKE THE UTTERLY UNLIKE

For Jews and Christians and all who know the God of the Bible, the Bible's view of humanity is unique for its strong insistence on human freedom and responsibility (with the repeated insistence that to be fully free, humans must be set free). The distinctiveness flows from its starting point—the Genesis declaration that humans are created in the image and likeness of God (Genesis 1:26-27). All human beings are profoundly shaped and influenced by their "country, culture, and kin," as it used to be said. But as Abraham heard, the call to follow God is the call to leave his country, culture, and kin and to break with all the routine determining forces.

No human being is ever to be solely determined like a puppet, whether determined by their stars, their karma, their genes, or any other external causation. Created in the image of God, every single human being is unique, precious, and unsubstitutable for any other human being. God, Creator of all that is, transcends the world of time and space that he has created, so he cannot and must not be represented by any created image—except one: the human creatures made in his image and likeness. Thus, we humans are *like the absolutely unlike*. Being God-*like*, we are not God, but being *God*-like, we are more than animals. We humans are never simply "toolmakers," "naked apes," "genes seeking to perpetuate themselves," or any such description based on our place in the natural world alone. Created in the image of God, we can only be truly understood and fulfilled by viewing ourselves upward and not downward.

This starting point underlies the character of human freedom in the Bible. Made in the image of God, we are free in ways that are both like and unlike God. God is sovereign and free; he has executive power and is free to exert his will despite all possible interference and opposition to his will.

We humans are neither sovereign nor absolutely free, but created in the image of God we are significant and free. As individuals we can express and exert our will in ways that decisively affect reality and shape history, for which we are responsible and accountable because we are free and not completely determined. Real freedom is what makes possible real change and real growth. Alone among the life forms on the earth, we are created with the ability to choose decisively and consequentially. We are most ourselves when we regard each other and treat each other as free and responsible human beings.

Consider four places where the Bible's insistence on human freedom is clear and emphatic. First, according to the Bible's account the truth of human freedom and responsibility begins with the astonishing fact that the first humans were free and able to choose to follow their own will rather than God's. The first sin, the source of original sin, was the expression of original freedom. For Adam and Eve to do wrong was a dishonor to their humanity, but their ability to do wrong was a compliment to their freedom. The very right to be wrong spelled freedom, or we might say misspelled freedom. It is certainly true that as God sets us free and transforms us, it is even greater freedom to become able not to sin, but to be able to sin is freedom. As all parents discover sooner or later, we are like God in that, in our love, we create children who grow to be free and independent people we can't and don't want to control.

Second and equally remarkably, God addressed humans as free even after they had sinned and asserted their freedom in open defiance of him. Freedom was not lost entirely after the fall. God warned Cain of the real-life consequences of the choice he was pondering in his heart and was about to make—"If you do well . . ." God said, and "If you do not do well . . ." (Genesis 4:7). It was a warning about a genuinely decisive and responsible choice that Cain faced. As the account continues, Cain listened to God's warning, freely brushed it aside, and made his own choice—with dire consequences as he was warned. God took seriously both his freedom and his responsibility.

Third, God continues to respect human freedom and responsibility down through history in always addressing humans with a choice as he confronts them. When Israel had been freed from Egypt and was about to enter their own land, God put their whole future before them as a matter of their choice and responsibility. He had freed them from slavery, and he had offered them a new way of relating to him, but they still had to play their part. They must agree to the covenant he set out, and they must keep on keeping their agreement. They must choose, they must keep on choosing, and they would be responsible for the choices they would make.

> See, I have set before you today life and prosperity, and death and adversity. . . . I call heaven and earth to witness against you today, that I have set before you life and death, the blessing and the curse. So choose life in order that you may live, you and your descendants. (Deuteronomy 30:15, 19)

God addressed his people as set free and able to choose. The overall choice was genuinely a choice, and they were

free to choose. There would be real consequences because
it was a real choice, and they were responsible because they
made it freely.

Fourth, and most intriguingly, the importance of freedom
is conveyed in the meaning of the profound way in which
humans are invited to come to know God and relate to God.
Unlike the gods of Greece, Rome, and paganism in general,
who are part of the forces of nature, the God of the Bible is
the Creator of nature and is outside nature, and he can never
be seen. He can only be heard. He speaks, and we humans
are to listen. The verbal is more important than the visual.
As the rabbis point out, the Torah famously contains 613
specific commands, but Hebrew has no word for "obey."
There is no equivalent of a word such as *Islam* (submission)
and no concept such as blind obedience. The nearest word
in Hebrew is *shema*, "listen," which has a richness not captured by the English word. To listen in Hebrew is not simply
to hear with the ear, physically and passively. Listening is not
blind obedience. To listen means to engage actively, to pay
attention and pay heed, to reflect and to deliberate before
responding freely. In sum, to listen is to relate to God with
the full attention of free and responsible human beings who
are created in his image and likeness and are set free; they
are most themselves when standing tall as free and responsible before him.

It is also true that our actions may seriously impair our
freedom. But put these four points together and you can see
that the Jewish and Christian understanding of freedom is
momentous. It is too easily taken for granted in countries that
pride themselves on freedom as their birthright but forget

where freedom came from. Yet now that so many modern thinkers deny that we humans are free, the biblical view is once again growing clearer by contrast. This conviction of freedom is titanic because freedom is essential for a host of reasons. Viewed negatively, for example, freedom means the right to do wrong and the freedom to destroy freedom. Thus, the paradox of freedom, whereby freedom can become the greatest enemy of freedom. Viewed positively, freedom means the possibility of creativity, growth, and change. Without a solid ground for freedom we will quickly be back in the world of chance, determinism, and resignation. Only with genuine freedom can there be genuine growth, genuine change, and genuine transformation—including the freedom to change ourselves and to change the world.

The personal challenge in freedom is plain. Not for one moment are we self-made human beings. We cannot be ourselves by ourselves. Not even the most prodigious egotist or entrepreneurial trillionaire can do that. We are dependent on God and other people every second of our lives, from our conception until the day we die. At the same time, human freedom means creativity. We are all artists in the sense that through our own free choices each of us for better or worse is fashioning our greatest creation in life—our selves and our characters.

Our generation knows more about genes, chemistry, and childhood influences than any generation has ever known, and some people face far greater difficulties and inequalities in life than others. But for all of us, freedom means that we need not remain who we were when we were born or who we are today. Set free, we can change. We can grow. We can be transformed.

We will never be perfect, but what we are making ourselves to be comes before any other contribution we might make to the world outside us, whether raising a family, writing a song, building a company, or reaching out in compassion to someone in need. Only if freedom is genuine can we trust that objectives such as *transforming ourselves* and *changing the world* will rise above slogans to become reality.

Contrast is again the mother of clarity, and the differences are no idle differences. For those who have put their trust in the God of the Bible, in contrast to such alternative philosophies as secularism, neither chance nor necessity has the decisive say in either the cosmos or our human affairs. Life is not fate. Freedom is a God-given gift and priceless. We humans may well make a wreck of our freedom. We may even end in bondage, but God does not take back his gift. All human beings are created for a life of freedom and responsibility, and we can be set free to live free.

Living under our own vine and fig tree is for those who live with freedom and responsibility in their self-understanding, their relationships, and their dealings—always aware of where their freedom comes from, always knowing who they are accountable to, and always grateful for their ultimate grounding in One who is more sure than life itself.

THE ESSENTIALS OF LIFE

BASIC REQUIREMENTS FOR FREEDOM

LET THEM EAT cake!" Marie Antoinette's infamous rejoinder to the news that the French peasants were starving and had no bread is almost certainly apocryphal, but it highlights a crucial lesson in the story of freedom. There can be no freedom unless the essentials of life are taken care of first. If the necessities of life are not in place for society as a whole or for some people within the society, freedom is limited for everyone. Any talk of freedom that remains will be exposed as hollow and hypocritical—a defense of privilege and reinforcement of inequality and injustice. The reason is that while the desire to be free is irrepressibly human, the desire to live is more basic still, and the need for the basics of life must be satisfied if freedom is to be given its place.

To live under our own vine and fig tree must never be a fancy rationale for excusing inhuman living conditions or for the injustice that allows some people to thrive at the expense of the poverty or the suffering of others. This warning should need no underscoring to Americans in light of America's shameful acceptance of racism and slavery along with the claims and celebrations of freedom. Samuel Johnson nailed the hypocrisy with pinpoint accuracy at the very time of the American Revolution. It was as clear as the day even an ocean away. "How is it," he said, "that we hear the loudest yelps for liberty among those who are drivers of negroes?" But it is worth considering the lesson as a foundational principle that challenges us all.

FIRST THINGS FIRST

This insistence on justice in terms of the necessities of life is prominent throughout the Bible. It is central to the Jewish and Christian understanding of freedom and justice, beginning most strikingly with the story of the Hebrew exodus. Even the greatest liberation in history must respect the prior human need for the essentials of life, though of course the greatest liberation in history was on behalf of such essentials—God in his freedom frees his people to worship and serve him freely and live together in freedom. This practical point is clear at the very start. Moses repeatedly tries to evade God's call because, as he says, he is not a good speaker, so the people will not listen. He is right that they will not listen but wrong that it was due to his lack of eloquence. The account describes their response to his appeal, "they did not listen to Moses on account of their despondency and cruel bondage" (Exodus 6:9). In other words, their liberation would have to address their physical situation if their spirit and will were to prove capable of following Moses to freedom. As Maimonides was to stress centuries later in *The Guide for the Perplexed,* no one can think spiritual thoughts or enjoy freedom if they are starving or sick, homeless and alone—or in captivity.

The same point is clear even when the Israelites had won their initial freedom from Pharaoh. By then the Israelites had seen more miracles in a short time than most nations are privileged to see in centuries. They had been liberated from slavery under the most powerful empire of their day and then, facing certain annihilation, they were given a miraculous passage through the Red Sea to safety. But after all the signs and wonders they had witnessed, they still started to complain the moment they were short of water or lacked meat in their diet. They were behaving as if no miracles had ever happened and as if God and Moses were expected to produce a miracle a day to satisfy their every longing. The initial complaint was the overture to their loud chorus of grumblings as they crossed the desert, and they are often accused of rank ingratitude and abject slave-mindedness. Yet their concerns were legitimate even if their complaints were wrong. To run out of water in the desert would be a death sentence, and to be suddenly attacked by a hostile tribe when they were only weeks from slavery and had no fighting army was a deadly threat to their existence.

But in fact these incidents illustrate the first two of three staples that the Israelites needed to survive and the necessities that any people need to thrive—and that God respected.

Leon Kass describes it well in his fascinating commentary *Founding God's Nation.* First, to be a people at rest, they needed sustenance—the necessities of life, which God answered through the provision of the manna and the quails. Second, to keep their enemies at bay, they needed defense against external attack, which was answered by Moses' prayer and through Joshua's command of the fighting forces. And third, to be a community at peace, they needed wise ordering—internal peace and order, which Moses's father-in-law, Jethro, answered through his suggestion that Moses delegate his leadership to serve the people better and not overtax himself.

The exodus account is spare, and it hurries over the details, but there is a set of ideals that is an early and community version of Abraham Maslow's "hierarchy of needs"—the people at rest, their enemies at bay, and the community at peace—and a corresponding set of practical requirements to match the ideals—the sustenance, the defense, and the ordering.

GOD CARES EVEN IF OTHERS DON'T

Overcoming these challenges was an early test of Israel's new freedom, but the lesson is clear. There are necessities of life that are essential to a people's survival and growth. Later when Israel had entered its own land and had grown into a successful and powerful nation, a similar concern became a test of Israel's loyalty to its covenant and its ideals of freedom and justice. It was therefore another test of its survival, but in a different sense. At the very heart of the Sinai covenant was the command "You shall love your neighbor as yourself" (Leviticus 19:18). This meant the equal dignity of all Jews and the reciprocal responsibility of all Jews for all their fellow Jews. Thus, justice as God required it was far more than institutional and procedural—a matter of the law and law courts. Justice was double-barreled. It was personal and relational as well as public and institutional. Justice was all about the way each person dealt with all other persons in the community, and God had an eye for those who were overlooked by others, so that even when no one else cared, God cared. (The grounds for "Injustice anywhere is a threat to justice everywhere.")

Famously, the Lord had a special eye for the poor, the widows, the orphans, and for all who were weak, powerless, left out, and unable to stand up for themselves. Justice was indivisible, and wherever power and privilege divided some and excluded others, freedom was abused and God was outraged. "Hear this," the prophet Amos thundered,

> you who trample the needy, to do away with the humble
> of the land. . . .
>
> So as to buy the helpless for money,
> And the needy for a pair of sandals. (Amos 8:4, 6)

Power abused is freedom abused, and freedom abused is injustice and evil.

This same concern sounded out equally clearly in the teaching of Jesus. How, for example, will God as King distinguish and decide between the sheep and the goats on the great Day of Judgment? The difference will be, the King replied, that the sheep will be favored because they gave him something to eat when he was hungry, something to drink when he was thirsty, and something to wear when he was naked. But when did we ever see you like that, the disciples ask surprised, and Jesus answers: "The King will answer and say to them, 'Truly I say to you, to the extent that you did it to one of these brothers of Mine, *even* the least *of them*, you did it to Me'" (Matthew 25:40). The way we treat our fellow humans is the ultimate demonstration of our belief that our fellow humans are, like us, all made in the image of God.

This third foundation stone, the conviction about justice and the necessities of life, is highly challenging. It must never be left out of current discussions of freedom if freedom is not to become a matter of privilege, a luxury for some at the expense of others. Freedom, like justice, is indivisible. We humans have power over nature and our fellow creatures, the animals, but with the exception of parents, whose love should limit their power, no human should ever have power over another human without their explicit or implicit consent. To exercise such power without consent is abuse, and for any human to abuse another human is an abuse of power and a violation of freedom.

If the great quest is the search for the meaning of life that makes possible a life worthy of life, then the great political task is the establishment of a way of community life that justifies, promotes, and safeguards the human spirit and therefore human dignity, freedom, justice, peace, and stability—and does so by putting moral limits on power.

Is there any question that the glaring violation of this principle lies at the heart of America's tragedy and current political contentions? *Never was freedom elevated so high and for so many as in 1776 and the Declaration of Independence, and never was freedom for all denied so blatantly and so cruelly as in the continuing slavery of captive Africans.* Can there be atonement for such an evil, or must the political system that produced it be replaced by another political system with a different view of freedom and justice? That question will arise later, but the principle of justice over essentials must be registered here with clarity. For any society or nation the ultimate goal at the collective level is to keep citizens at rest, to keep enemies at bay, and to keep the community at peace. But since freedom is not the end but the means, the first necessity is to take care of the basics of human existence. Unless the basic human necessities are in place, talk of freedom will always seem like a luxury rather than a necessity. Freedom will sound like "Let them eat cake" when what our neighbors and fellow humans need is bread.

ORDERING FREEDOM

MAXIMIZING FREEDOM AND RESPONSIBILITY FOR EVERYONE

I**F EACH OF US** wants to be free and we recognize that other people want to be free too, how do we organize society so that everyone can be as free as possible without bumping into each other or descending into chaos? If freedom is essential for human beings to be fully themselves, how should things be run so that every member of society enjoys that same freedom and everyone can live together freely?

A whole cluster of issues lies behind these simple-sounding questions. The traditional way is to survey the different models of societies and governments that humans have devised down the centuries. But those opening questions would surprise most people in history at once. Aristotle, for example, was often reported to have thanked Fortune for three things: "first, that I am a human and not a beast; second, that I am a man and not a woman; third, that I am a Greek and not a barbarian." The great Greek philosopher took it for granted that the laws of society should be directly in line with the laws of nature, and that nature provided no grounds for either liberty or equality for all.

Plato had looked at humanity and judged that some humans were like gold, some like silver, and some like bronze, and society should reflect these differences. There was no equality in nature, so equality in society would not be natural or right. His disciple, Aristotle, thought the same thing. Aristotle taught in his *Politics* how natural it was that some humans were born to rule and others to be ruled. "That one should command, and others obey, is not just necessary but expedient." Was there any question that the gods ruled the cosmos, the sun ruled the heavens, and the lion was king of the animals? It was surely natural and right, then, that a society should be ruled by a king, an emperor, a pharaoh, or at least by an excellent elite. The idea of freedom and equality for everyone was simply not in their thinking. It would have been considered naive and even dangerous.

With assumptions like that in many different forms across the world, it is hardly surprising that for societies that went beyond the organic, like families, and were not linked by blood and kinship, the predominant form of society in history was hierarchical. If there is any element of agreement in a hierarchical society, it is a one-way agreement that is imposed and not free. Hierarchical societies are based on power, and power comes from the top down. The sky-topping Babylonian ziggurat at Ésagila and the massive grandeur of the Great Pyramid of Khufu at Giza were perfect statements of hierarchical power in brick and stone. Broad at the base and narrow at the top, the god-man or the man-god who was king, pharaoh, or emperor was the top stone that rested on all the stones below, and all the stones below were there to support and serve the top stone. One man alone was supreme, and the lower the others below him, the less they mattered. Legend has it that when the Tower of Babel was being built, there was an outcry when a brick was wasted or destroyed, but none at all when human life was lost.

The same was true in imperial China and imperial Japan, and the situation is no different under the totalitarian China of Mao Zedong or Xi Jinping. Early in the twentieth century my grandfather who was a Cambridge-educated doctor was invited into the Forbidden City in Peking (now Beijing) during the reign of the Empress Dowager. He was horrified to witness what happened one day when a nervous and unfortunate serving girl spilled some tea. She was at once taken out to a well, thrust down headfirst, and left to die. Life under the pharaohs, emperors, caesars, tsars, and party secretaries of the ages has always been cheap. As Stalin remarked cynically, the death of an individual is a tragedy; the death of millions is a statistic.

The Greeks, of course, and following them the Romans, set the pattern for how we sort out different governments. They divided governments and societies into three categories— monarchy, the rule of one; aristocracy, the rule of the excellent few; and democracy, the rule of the people. In their realism they well knew that the wheel turns and neither life nor politics are stable. Each ideal form of government had a corrupt form (tyranny, oligarchy, and mob rule). Tellingly, all but one of the six types are hierarchical in one way or another, and hierarchical societies, based on power, are inherently coercive and inevitably grow corrupt and end in oppression. Even democracy descends to the rule of power when it is corrupted into the rule of the mob. Societies with the ideal of liberty and equality for all are rare.

The alternative to the increasing rarity of organic societies and to the corruptible, power-based hierarchical model is a third model with two different forms: the contractual society and the covenantal society. Scholars have long recognized three basic forms of relationships within society. Pitirim Sorokin called them the "familistic," the "compulsory," and the "contractual." More recently, Jewish scholar Daniel Elazar revised the classical Greek and Roman categories by shifting the focus from governments and the ruling of societies to the founding of societies. Seen this new way, a large number of societies are again *hierarchical*, based on power, as evident down through the ages. Others are *organic*, based on ties of blood and kinship, such as families, clans, tribes, medieval society, and modern Near Eastern countries such as Lebanon. But what Elazar explored was a third and rarer type of society—*contractual* or *covenantal*, based on a free and common binding agreement between the people.

Ordinary contractual relationships are very common—for example, between sellers and buyers, employers and employees, landlords and tenants, and so on. The key feature of contractual relationships is that they are all about the overlapping interests of the parties, and they are very specific and limited in what they cover and how long they last. The parties to the contract matter to each other, but not as people in their own right. The parties are simply people whose mutual interests are served by the contract. The contract expresses the specific interests of the parties, who desire some specific benefits, but it says nothing about their overall relationship or how they are to behave in the rest of their lives.

Contracts express the rights and duties with great care in order to limit the liability. Legally, contracts are a matter of *no more and no less.* At their worst, since contracts are all about interests, they can be a way of one party seeking to get as much as possible for as little as possible from the other side.

Covenants are the highest form of contract but also very different. They lift the principle of voluntary agreement to a higher plane and a broader level. They move the parties from a practical calculation to a moral commitment, from a matter of pure individual self-interest to collective partnership in a project, and thus from a potentially egotistical "I" to a genuinely collective "We the people." Covenants are not unique to the Bible, and there are different covenants in the Bible, but the greatest and most influential covenant in history is the covenant between God and the Israelite nation agreed upon at Mount Sinai. This was the founding constitution of the Jewish people, and centuries later, following the Reformation and its principle of *sola Scriptura*, covenantalism came to have a profound impact on modern notions of freedom. Switzerland, the Netherlands, Scotland, England, and above all the United States were all influenced in different ways by the precedent and pattern of the Hebrew republic. It is extraordinary how few Americans realize that the US Constitution is a nationalized and somewhat secularized form of the Hebrew covenant.

At the heart of the Sinai covenant are three principles that proved revolutionary for freedom. First, the covenant was a matter of *freely chosen consent*. Three times the Israelites responded to God's proposal, "All that the LORD has spoken we will do." This statement is the origin of the crucial principle of the consent of the governed. The result was what Michael Walzer at Princeton University has called an "almost democracy," and the basic language of politics in a free society shifts from coercion to persuasion and consent.

Second, the Sinai covenant was *a morally binding pledge*. Far more than a legal contract, narrow and binding only in a limited area, the covenant was comprehensive and lasting and covered the scope of Israelite society. It depended on a promise given and a promise kept, and in that sense a covenant is essentially an exchange of promises that creates a depth of relationship and promotes trust. The fruitfulness of a marriage covenant between a husband and a wife is obvious, but the same is true of citizenship within a nation—citizens within a covenant keep trust with other citizens over the commonly agreed ideals they share as a nation.

Third, the Sinai covenant was a matter of *the reciprocal responsibility of everyone for everyone*. The covenant the Israelites agreed to was both a covenant with God and a covenant with all other Jews. Famously, they were commanded to love their neighbors as themselves (Leviticus 19:18), so that "every Jew was responsible for every Jew." A community, a society, or a nation is simply a term for the total of all the human relationships within it. The result of a covenantal community was therefore a collective authority, a mutual responsibility, and a national solidarity—all of it centuries before France's Three Musketeers' "One for all and all for one," and the historic words of the US Constitution, "We the people."

This reciprocal responsibility is vital to a covenantal-constitutional society such as the American republic. It means there is always a common good to balance the individualism, a *unum* to be forged from the *pluribus*. As Jefferson wrote in his *Memoir and Correspondence*, "A nation as a society forms a moral person, and every member of it is personally responsible for his society." A covenantal-constitutional republic means a politics of all Americans together, with no single American exempt. Just as history must not be outsourced to Google and Wikipedia, so citizenship must not be delegated to activists, consultants, pollsters, and lobbyists. If the American republic is to survive, every American is responsible for America.

DISTINCTIVE BUT NOT EXCEPTIONAL

Needless to say, the differences between the types of society and the types of relationships are not cast iron and immutable. But it is clear that the rich dimensions of covenantalism that once inspired the US Constitution have slackened and slumped into contractualism. For a start, America is in serious danger of minimizing the importance of citizenship. Civic education has been expelled from the public schools, the southern border has been open indiscriminately to all comers, the focus of voting in elections has shifted from the casting of votes to the counting of votes, and New York Democrats have taken the lead in allowing noncitizens to vote along with citizens. In sum, America is a covenantal-constitutional republic in name only, and the citizenship a republic requires is becoming a relic of the past.

Many Americans have no idea where their Constitution came from, and how a covenant is different from a contract. They have lost all sense of the distinctiveness of their covenantal-constitutional form of government and what it means and requires. Oddly, they pride themselves on American exceptionalism, when in fact the claim to be exceptional is anything but exceptional—every great superpower has considered itself exceptional in its own way. But they fail to understand their true distinctiveness—and above all its roots in the Hebrew republic and its responsibilities for American freedom today. Many Americans, for example, cite the importance of the rule of law as a bulwark of freedom, but they press no deeper. The rule of law is vital for all democratic societies. It is one of the vital principles that allows them to steer clearly between the Scylla of anarchy and the Charybdis of authoritarianism.

The role of the rule of law is obvious in avoiding anarchy. Without law, or the rules by which the game is played and not played, society quickly descends into chaos, conflict, and violence. Individualism run rampant leads to chaos. Everyone does what is right in their own eyes and the devil take the hindmost. But the rule of law is equally important in staving off authoritarianism, as anyone doing business in communist China would tell you.

That much about the rule of law should be clear, but there is a deeper and equally important question to be asked. Why should anyone respect and obey the law? Why should anyone be law-abiding? There are three major answers to this question, and only one of the three favors and maximizes freedom.

The first answer is based on the principle of power and is therefore natural to hierarchical societies with compulsory relationships. The law must be obeyed as a command of the will of the ruler or rulers, and those who do not obey will be punished. Hierarchical power coerces. The desire not to be punished will be enough to avoid anarchy, but it fits in too well with authoritarianism, and such hierarchical power by itself will always be corrupted. That is not the way of freedom.

The second answer is based on the principle of self-interest and is therefore natural to contractual societies. We are to obey the law because it is in our best interests to do so, whether the law is a matter of respecting traffic lights, paying income taxes, or not assaulting other people. The trouble is that in a purely contractual society certain individuals may pursue their self-interest amorally and aggressively so that self-interest becomes a form of rampant egotism, greed, and ruthless exploitation that leaves freedom, justice, equality, and the common good in tatters. That too is not the way of freedom.

The third answer is the one that favors freedom. The law, passed by a parliament or congress of freely chosen people, is to be obeyed as a freely chosen moral and voluntary undertaking—a free and responsible pledge by free people. This answer combines the force of the first covenant principle of "freely chosen consent" with the force of the second covenant principle of "the morally binding pledge," and thus achieves the third covenant principle, "the reciprocal responsibility of all for all." Thus, properly understood, freedom is a moral matter and a covenant is broader, deeper, and richer than a contract. Follow the ideas of Hobbes and Rousseau and you forge a contract that creates a state, but follow the ideas of Mount Sinai and you forge a covenant that creates a free and just society.

STRENGTHS AND WEAKNESSES

Needless to say, systems of human government and rationales for the rule of law are no more perfect than we humans ourselves, so every system and every rationale have their strengths and weaknesses. The strength and weakness of the covenantal-constitutional model are as obvious as those of the others. On the one hand, the strength lies in the fact that covenantal societies represent the supreme form of ordered freedom, maximizing both freedom and responsibility. The covenantal-constitutional vision of society holds the promise of the greatest trust, freedom, and relational richness found in any social and political system in history. From the initial consent on, the terms of the covenant provide the greatest opportunity for both individuals and the community as a whole to exercise and negotiate both freedom and responsibility. With the covenant comes pledging, with pledging comes promise-keeping, with promise-keeping comes trust, and with trust comes freedom. This means that when there is high trust there can be high freedom—which is in striking contrast to other forms of government where low trust means low freedom and the need for high control and high surveillance.

On the other hand, the weakness of covenantal-constitutional societies is also obvious in the unreliability of human promise-keeping. God has stood by his covenant and kept faith with Israel "for a thousand generations." But again and again there was a breakdown on Israel's side—and on America's part today. Think of the kneeling controversy and its deliberate disrespect of the anthem, the flag, the pledge, the Declaration of Independence, and the ideals they point to. Martin Luther King Jr. fought against the same evils as Colin Kaepernick, but Dr. King looked to the Declaration of Independence as a "promissory note" that should now be cashed in, whereas the kneelers have rejected it as hypocrisy. Thinkers from Machiavelli to David Hume have long pointed out that humans can't be trusted to keep promises. So, unless the promise-keeping and the pledge-making are cultivated and guarded with great care, in families and schools, societies that are based on freely chosen consent, expressed in promises and pledges, will always be vulnerable to drift, breakdown, and decline.

The cultural climate change mentioned earlier has played a deadly role here. Philosophical cynicism destroys truth and objectivity, moral corruption undermines integrity and justice, and social collapse works its way through institutions such as the family because of the dissolving ties and bonds. Truth and trust have died in postmodern America, and freedom is now dying too. People who think that the real world consists only of dollars and cents, or missiles and majorities, will discount this sort of thinking as soft-headed and sentimental. But the truth is that the integrity that is loyalty to our word is quite literally the foundation of all human relationships, from a small family to a large nation. Promise-keeping is an indispensable necessity for freedom and a good society.

Think back to the bookends of history. Anarchy is unlivable, so there is little question that America's breakdown of covenantal-constitutional freedom will lead to authoritarianism in the end. The lure of Leviathan is abroad in the world. On the eve of the First World War, H. G. Wells published the last of his three "fantasias of possibility," *The World Set Free*. He imagined an "epidemic of sanity" breaking out on the earth as world leaders realized that humanity was faced with the horrendous prospect of the discovery of limitless power, endless nationalisms, and increasingly destructive wars. Meeting together in a "last desperate effort to save humanity," their solution was obvious—a "World Republic," the creation of global "Intelligence," and the subordination of all individual interests to "the collective future." The only way to save humanity was through cosmocracy. "There's got to be one simple government for all the world. . . . Manifestly war has to stop forever. . . . Manifestly this can only be done by putting all the world under one government." As for the people in the New World Order, "The governed will show their consent by silence."

It would be easy to trace the line from H. G. Wells before the Great War to Stefan Zweig at the end, and down to such contemporary leaders as George Soros and Klaus Schwab. Each of them would have their own rationale for world government. If Adolf Hitler had won the war, it would have been a *Pax Teutonica*. Arnold Toynbee's gentler vision would have been a *Pax Oecumenica*. What matters as much as the differences are the recurring themes—the resort to globalism, the reliance on collectivism, the faith in science and intelligence (Wells: "Where should we be now but for the grace of science?"), the expressions of utopianism, and the thrusting assertiveness of humanism (Wells: "Very soon now, old Sun, I shall launch myself at you, and I shall reach you and I shall put my foot on your spotted face and tug you about by your fiery locks"). Those who reject the simplicity and contentment of living under their own vine and fig tree may soon find themselves as conscripts slaving on the construction of the grand new global Tower of Babel. But the covenant model still stands as the better way to a society with freedom and justice for all.

10

FREEDOM, THE GREATEST ENEMY OF FREEDOM

REALISM AND THE NEED FOR SAFEGUARDS AGAINST THE ABUSE OF FREEDOM

FOR THE GREAT German philosopher Georg Wilhelm Friedrich Hegel, history was not random, and it was far more than the record of past events. In his *Lectures on the Philosophy of World History* in 1822, he argued that there is a purpose and meaning to history, and it lies in the unfolding progress of the consciousness of freedom. What he called "the spirit of the world" was unveiled in the course of great events and the achievements of great men. Unfortunately, however, the climax of freedom as he saw it in his time was the spirit of the French Revolution ("a glorious mental dawn") and the "great-man" triumph of Napoleon Bonaparte, whom he called a "world soul on horseback" (brilliantly captured in Jacques-Louis David's heroic painting of the titanic French conqueror and the scourge of Europe). Yet if Napoleon epitomized the progress of human freedom, then clearly freedom was power, spectacular, irresistible power. And what meant power and glory for some meant defeat, domination, and death and destruction for many others. Hegel's freedom, in short, ended as so many quests for freedom do, in authoritarianism.

Freedom, to put it simply, can either be used or misused, and all who care about freedom must ask why freedom so often goes wrong, terribly wrong. It is one thing to be a human being and quite another to live up to being human. Freedom is the heart of being human, but the abuse of freedom is the heart of inhumanity. Fyodor Dostoevsky's famous conclusion in his novel *Demons* could be written over many revolutionary movements that aim for freedom but end in oppression: "Starting from unlimited freedom, I conclude with unlimited despotism."

The irony is stark. We humans, it appears, may aim for freedom individually and end in addiction or as prodigals in a pigsty. We may struggle for freedom collectively and drive our revolutions toward totalitarianism. In seeking to be angels, we may become beasts. In striving to be as God, we can degenerate into devils. Behind such ironic outcomes lies the question of human nature. Are we humans naturally good, or are we naturally bad? Are we altruistic or are we selfish? Thinkers down the centuries have debated these questions, and the different answers have led to different politics. Thomas Hobbes, for example, provided the rationale for many on the conservative side. He looked on the darker side of human nature and argued that Leviathan, the "mortal god" of the state, was the only way to control the instinctive conflict of power that would otherwise end in death. Loss of freedom is the price of security. Jean-Jacques Rousseau, on the other hand, was a leading philosopher behind the French Revolution. He believed that we humans are naturally good. It is only our society and our institutions that make us bad, which justifies the revolutionary violence that it takes to overthrow them. In the common refrain of radicals, "To make an omelet, you have to break eggs." Use whatever means it takes to remove the chains, and then we will all be happy, free, and fulfilled.

Michael Oakeshott, the distinguished political philosopher, in his essay on *Leviathan* offers this pithy summary: "The nature of man is the predicament of mankind."

THE PARADOX OF FREEDOM

The Bible's position on human nature is different from both of these extremes and distinctive for its combination of utter realism and unconquerable hope. There is no higher view of human worth than the Bible's and no lower view of the depth to which humans can sink than the Bible's. Created in the image of God, but choosing to go against God's will, we are capable of soaring grandeur and heart-searing rottenness. We can be strikingly creative and horrifyingly destructive. Our capacity for both good and evil is remarkable, and it can lead as easily to sorrow, outrage, and shame as to wonder and admiration. There is an almost cosmic ambivalence in humanity, and realism in appreciating it should form the backdrop for understanding freedom and its enduring conundrum. Simplistic views of freedom are naive and dangerous. Self-righteousness, the pride that turns a blind eye to our own faults, is one of the deadliest dangers to freedom. Freedom is as easily misused and abused as used well, and the double-edged character of freedom requires both constant respect and constant vigilance.

Our individual experiences of life will naturally sway us in one direction or another in shaping our confidence in humanity and change. There are Westerners with unbounded confidence in human goodness and perfectibility, people for whom evil is unreal and freedom is effortless. They were born with a silver spoon in their mouths, and the dark side of life is as remote as a headline in a newspaper or an incident in a quickly forgotten film. There are others for whom an experience of darkness is indelible and the pain relentless. The issue between the two becomes real in a sphere such as politics where naivety and utopianism are dangerous. I, for one, am European, and though I was born in China, I was educated and came of age in Europe. The history of wars, colonialism, and the knowledge of the death camps made the reality of human depravity inescapable, but the glory of the great cathedrals and the genius of great creators such as Dante, Michelangelo, Shakespeare, Rembrandt, and Mozart made human creativity equally real. The paradox is vivid and self-evident in Europe.

Earlier, I had lived my first ten years in China—in a war in which seventeen million were killed in an invasion, in a famine in which five million died in three months (including my two brothers), in a city that experienced the most brutal massacre of the twentieth century (the rape of Nanking), and in a reign of terror that was an overture to a revolution that may have killed up to seventy-five million people (the Chinese revolution in 1949 under Mao Zedong). For any who have witnessed such realities, the experience inoculates the mind against falling for any facile revolutionary promise to change the world through political action. Indeed, the memory underscores the warning that runs through this book: *the revolutions of the left never succeed, and their oppression never ends.*

There is a simple way to build a wise realism about the potent promise of freedom, and that is to explore the great paradox of freedom: *the paradox of freedom is the fact that the greatest enemy of freedom is freedom.* The truth is that no one and nothing enslaves free people as much as they enslave themselves. The paradox can be observed from several angles. First, considered historically, free societies have failed again and again—when freedom runs to excess and breeds permissiveness and license, when people who love freedom so love to be safe and secure in their freedom that their love of security undermines their freedom, and when free societies become so caught up in the glory of freedom that they justify anything and everything done in its name, including things that quite clearly contradict freedom.

Second, considered politically, freedom is not self-sustaining. As the French philosopher Montesquieu insisted, freedom requires both the *structures* of freedom, such as a covenant-constitution and laws, and the *spirit* of freedom. Yet the tendency, alas, is to rely on the former and forget the latter and so to lose both.

Third, considered ethically, freedom requires a framework. (*It is not the permission to do what we like, but the power to do what we ought.*) Freedom requires order and restraint—what Edmund Burke called "chains on the appetites" and Lord Moulton called "obedience to the unenforceable." But this restraint is the very thing that freedom undermines when it flourishes.

And fourth, considered spiritually and psychologically, freedom requires a responsibility that can be considered a burden and even a cause of suffering. At some point in the dark labyrinths where we humans rationalize our evasions of responsibility, things become twisted. People who desire to evade responsibility get to the point where there appears to be tyranny in freedom because of its responsibility, and freedom in tyranny, because there is no responsibility required, only dependency. The result grows into a fear of freedom that ends in a desire for freedom from freedom.

Americans should use these four angles to assess the state of the Union today. Is freedom in a healthy condition? Or are there signs of the paradox emerging again? After World War II, Erich Fromm's *Escape from Freedom* was the book that opened many people's eyes to the paradox of freedom, but the Hebrew and Christian Scriptures demonstrated the same realism far earlier. In the words of Rabbi Sacks, "evil has two faces." One face is turned to the outside world, in what evil does to the victim. "The second—turned within—is what it does to its perpetrator. Evil traps the evildoer in its mesh. Slowly but surely he or she loses freedom and becomes not evil's master but its slave." Freedom is not a matter of either-or, Sacks concludes, but of more or less. There are degrees of freedom and degrees in losing freedom too. People can become truly free (as in the Declaration of Independence), and proudly trumpet their freedom (as on the Fourth of July). But they can still go on either to exert their freedom over others (the African slaves and the Native Americans) or in failing to rule over themselves they can still become slaves to their own chosen ideas (obsessions) and their own chosen behavior (addictions).

The paradox of freedom is sobering, but for those who would become free and stay free, it is essential. It is essential above all because it demonstrates yet again why it is that to be free we need to be set free. It is sobering too because there are obvious but false ways of responding. If freedom is rare and inherently fragile, it is inevitably insecure, so surely the obvious way to counter the insecurity is to surround ourselves with the glorious, the massive, and the lasting—in short, to make a bid for permanence through monumentalism in the pyramids of the pharaohs, the great walls of the emperors, the triumphal arches of the caesars, and the Grand Armées of the Napoleons. Yet all such "immortality projects," as Sacks reminds us, fall prey to the fate of Shelley's "Ozymandias." Better far realism about human nature and realism about the risk of human freedom. Free people must thrive on the risk and daring of sustaining freedom as freedom requires, beginning with the need to be set free.

RIGHTING WRONGS

RESTORING FREEDOM WHEN
MISUSED AND ABUSED

H OW SHOULD WRONGS be righted, especially national wrongs, so that whole people and whole societies can go forward freely into the future? How is injustice to be resolved when it becomes so egregious that it is said to be systemic and chronic and threatens to burst the very bounds of the rule of law? If, as Martin Luther King Jr. declared (quoting Theodore Parker a century earlier), "The arc of the moral universe is long, but it bends toward justice," what moral consequences and what judgments will justice exact in response to America's worst injustices?

Over what is now the greater part of American history, and certainly ever since the Civil War, the land of the free has been wrestling with its own history and conscience concerning those to whom Americans denied both freedom and justice in the appalling iniquity of chattel slavery. From the brooding eloquence of Abraham Lincoln down to the civil rights marches of Martin Luther King Jr., Andrew Young, John Lewis, and Rabbi Abraham Joshua Heschel, through the Berkeley Free Speech Movement, the anti–Vietnam War protests, and down to the #MeToo movement, Black Lives Matter, and critical race theory, America has fought the varied demons of its unresolved past in a myriad of ways. Sometimes the struggle has been successful, as in the heroic achievements of Lincoln and the civil rights movement. At other times it has been disastrous, as in the reverse racism of today's antiracism theories that are in danger of elevating race and blood in the same dangerous way that the Nazis did.

The conflicts are mounting again. After the killing of George Floyd, a Black man killed by a White police officer in Minneapolis in May 2020, riots were unleashed in America's streets and conflicts were unleashed in America's schools. It is plain that America is as far away from genuine resolution as ever. Will America's past bring down America's future? Is America's failure due to the just punishments of God, as Lincoln concluded, or due to blundering inadequacies in the attempted solutions? Why is there no resolution in sight? Will America still be paying its debts a century from now? The deepest reasons for the failure currently are, first, the conflict over the legacy of the two revolutions (1776 and 1789), and second, the fact that advanced modern America knows no way of putting wrongs right and therefore no effective means of going forward from its past with a clear conscience and a free future.

DELIVER OR DECLINE!

There is a reason why this unresolved problem is critical. Contrary to advocates of the 1619 Project, slavery and racism are not in the DNA of America's great experiment, but they are the absolute and fundamental contradiction to its DNA. So long as they continue unresolved the great experiment dooms itself. The only question is the time the doom takes to come. Arnold Toynbee, for example, interpreted the rise and fall of nations and civilizations according to his notion of "challenge, response, and breakdown." The word *breakdown* sounds ominous as it suggests the final end of something, but for Toynbee breakdown was not the end of a nation or civilization or even the beginning of the end but the end of the beginning. It was a faulty response to a challenge that was critical. It was therefore the decisive end of a nation or civilization's promising rise toward its full potential, and it spelled out the reason for the eventual decline of the nation, however far ahead in the future.

A nation or civilization that fails to respond well to such a fundamental challenge triggers a breakdown that, unless resolved, ensures the eventual decline of the nation or civilization. There can be no question that slavery and racism are that breakdown issue for America. First, the contradiction is the critical challenge that requires a decisive and adequate response if America is to be true to itself and fulfill its promise; second, the unresolved contradiction is the breeding ground for further rapidly multiplying contradictions that bog down the nation in troubles and guarantee its eventual decline.

Unlike all who view nations as organisms in nature that age and die inevitably, Toynbee had a high place for the

Jewish and Christian understanding of human freedom and responsibility. But that conviction of freedom simply sharpened the human responsibility for exercising freedom well. Without a satisfactory response to a challenge that is critical to its character, America simultaneously betrays itself and commits suicide—which of course is what the young Abraham Lincoln warned in his address at the Young Men's Lyceum at Springfield, Illinois, in 1838: "If destruction be our lot, we must ourselves be its author and finisher. As a nation of freemen, we must live through all time, or die by suicide."

The practical dilemma in dealing with wrongs is straightforward, whether the wrongs are trivial, as in a passing family quarrel, or as in America's case, nationally devastating. The challenge can be expressed in three options and three words: *accumulation*, *appeasement*, and *atonement*. The accumulation option is unlivable—to let the wrongs mount and mount unaddressed until they become a downward spiral of action, reaction, and further reaction that becomes unstoppable and destructive. The result is breakdown and divorce in a family or a Corsican blood feud of conflict and violence in a nation, with an ever-perpetuating cycle of violence, vengeance, and vendetta. The logic of this option leads directly to the bookend of anarchy. It is Hobbes's "war of all against all" or far earlier still the Bible's description of the violence of the world before the flood when God saw that "the wickedness of man was great on the earth, and that every intent of the thoughts of his heart was only evil continually" (Genesis 6:5). As always with extreme anarchy the outcome leads to violence and a desire for order rather than lawlessness and for control instead of chaos so that the bookend of anarchy drives people toward its opposite extreme: the bookend of authoritarianism.

If the first option, accumulation, is unlivable, the second option, appeasement, is unwelcome. It occurs when the party responsible for the wrongdoing is seen as too powerful to be challenged—whether the abuser in a family, a nation with overwhelming power, or the gods themselves as the pagans saw them. In the infamous words of the cynical ultimatum that Athens delivered to the tiny island of Melos in Thucydides' account of the Peloponnesian War, "The strong do what they can and the weak suffer what they must." When power is irresistible, the only option for the weaker party is either abasement, so that the weaker appears to be no threat to the stronger, or appeasement by one means or another, so that the weaker person gets back in the good graces of the stronger one. The result, of course, is authoritarianism and a complete loss of freedom once again as the stronger party prevails. The difference is that the logic of this option leads to the bookend of authoritarianism directly rather than indirectly as in the first option.

The third option, atonement, is the desirable option. It occurs when there is genuine resolution of the wrongs and reconciliation of the parties so that they are brought back together ("at one" again), enemies can become friends, and unity and freedom is restored. But how is this to happen? Here is where America has to make a crucial choice today. For anyone who pauses to think, it is clear that today's political establishment (the emerging oligarchy) has little or nothing to say in addressing moral wrongs and injustices. The worldview of the mainstream elites is purely secular, and their solutions are heavily technocratic, managerial, and therapeutic. When addressing America's wrongs as a moral evil, the choice comes down to the difference between the radical left and the Jewish and Christian approach to righting wrongs.

THE PEACE OF DESPOTISM

The radical left is the child of neo-Marxism or cultural Marxism. It claims to be a revolutionary liberationism that sets free all who are victimized, marginalized, and oppressed. Following the French *philosophes* Voltaire and Diderot and their animosity toward God and the church, the radical left is militantly hostile to faith in God. And following Nietzsche and the philosophy of postmodernism, the radical left is post-truth and opposed to such notions as truth, objective reality, and moral knowledge. Thus, without either God or truth the sole remaining principle of the radical left is power, and all that it does in analyzing and confronting evils and injustices is couched in terms of power. The ancient Romans complained about their monarchy that whatever their kings desired had the power of law. The same is true of today's authoritarians and America's radical left. No Jewish or Christian standards are allowed to stand in the way. All traditions can be flouted. Arbitrariness is the soul of authoritarianism. Whatever the authority says and does is at once made right and necessary by definition and by power. Unless this process is reversed, the collapse of the covenantal republic will be the story of the relentless alienation of the once inalienable.

There are many fuller critiques of the radical left (including my *The Magna Carta of Humanity: Sinai's Revolutionary Faith and the Future of Freedom*). But the essence of its approach is plain. First, the radical left analyzes social and political discourse or how a society or nation speaks about what it takes for granted as real and good. It aims to look for what the society considers the majority view and the minority view and above all who are the oppressors and who are the oppressed or victims. This analysis is called "critical theory" and is undertaken by "social justice scholars." Critical theory has many branches, such as critical women studies, critical race studies, critical queer studies, and so on. Second, the radical left or "social justice warriors" weaponizes the victims and uses them to attack, subvert, and overthrow the status quo in the name of liberation and revolution. The radical left in America is a form of cultural Marxism rather than classical Marxism or communism in that its tactics engage the cultural gatekeepers of society rather than radicalizing the proletariat and working to foment an industrial strike. But its endgame is the same: subversion and revolution.

No one should forget the endgame of the radical left. There are too many well-meaning people who know nothing about critical theory and its astute use of dog whistles and crossover words. They naively think that *woke* simply means "alert to injustice," so they adopt it for themselves and use it as a compliment for the young, the idealistic, and the kind. That is inexcusably foolish. To be sure, *woke* may indeed mean "alert to injustice"—which we should all be—but in the case of the left that is only half the story. *Woke* not only means "alert to injustice" but "active for revolution." Many a woke politician, woke journalist, woke CEO, woke teacher, woke pastor, and woke parent will wake up one day to realize they have sawn off the branch they were sitting on and swapped their freedom for despotism.

The verdict on the radical left and its claims of liberation on behalf of "liberty, fraternity, equality" is blunt and damning. *The revolutionary left never succeeds, and its oppression never ends.* The central reason is plain. Power (and coercion and violence) are the sole principles of operation, so the end justifies the means, and the means in turn shape the end. Two features of the outcome are especially noteworthy. One is the ruthlessness of the left. The left is merciless. There is no recognition of the presumption of innocence. Once accused, someone is guilty, and guilt by association and guilt by membership of a group or class is sufficient (whether the group is aristocrats in eighteenth-century France or Whites in twenty-first-century America). The result in 1789 was the rush to the guillotine and today an instant consignment to censorship and canceling, shaming, and statue toppling.

America in the last generation has shifted from an inner-directed society to an other-directed society, demonstrated for example in the obsession with opinion polls. There has also been an accompanying shift from a guilt culture to a shame culture. In a guilt culture a doer and his deed can be distinguished, so that the deed can be dealt with and the doer remains, whereas in a shame culture the doer and their deeds become fused, and the doer is judged and banished forever along with the condemnation of the misdeed.

The other inescapable feature of the radical left is unsurprising: authoritarianism. In setting up a conflict with no operating principles except power, the result can only be a conflict without end or what the Romans called "the peace of despotism." If power is the be-all and end-all in the conflict, only one peaceful outcome is possible—Caesarism, Big Brother, brownshirts, the jackboot, and the iron heel. There can only be peace when a power emerges that is victorious and unrivaled, a power so strong that it can put down all other powers. In short, the outcome of the revolutionary struggles of the radical left, whether classical or cultural Marxism, is the end of freedom and authoritarianism's encore. This outcome is no accident but the logical implication of the principles by which the radical left operates.

The point stated simply in the introduction now goes beyond America to cover the entire West. For a century and more, classical Marxism, in the form of the Russian Revolution of 1917, was the first great secession from Western civilization since the West rose to its dominance. That simple fact should make Americans think. In America now, cultural Marxism, in the form of the "long march through the institutions," is as drastic a secession from the American republic as the South was a decisive secession from the Union in the Civil War. Together the *red wave* created by the two forms of Marxism sounds the death knell of Christendom, the American republic, and Western civilization.

Pitirim Sorokin, the titanic Russian American social scientist, who in his youth was imprisoned by both the tsarist and the Bolshevik regimes, was scathing in denouncing the advocates of revolutionary progress. In his monumental survey of history, *Social and Cultural Dynamics*, he described what the radical left represented. Champions of freedom and justice? The vanguard of the future of humanity? No. No.

No. "These mobs and their leaders are the vultures that appear when the social and cultural body is decomposing. Their eternal historical function is to pull it to pieces, and thus, though involuntarily, to clear the ground for a new life. Creation is not given to them." Liberals who view the radical left as liberals with an excess of energy, who condone the riots as "peaceful protests," and who plaster their walls with Black Lives Matter slogans as a surrogate to cover their in-activism are in for a nasty surprise. In seeking to right America's wrongs, the victory of the radical left would rule out American freedom and democracy altogether.

LET MY PEOPLE GO!

The Jewish and Christian way, or the Bible's way, to put wrongs right is quite different and, strikingly, it serves the interests of freedom at every stage from beginning to end. The chief snag about this way, of course, is that many intelligent Americans have rejected it without thinking. They have branded it as "religious" or at best "private" and overlooked its highly practical and political significance. That is a fateful mistake because of the nature of America's crisis, which has an inescapable moral and spiritual dimension. The problem is not that such Americans have examined the Jewish and Christian way and then rejected it but that they have rejected it without examining it at all. All Americans should think again. It is not too much to say that when it comes to the dark legacy of slavery, racism, and the treatment of Native Americans, *America's greatest evil encounters the establishment's greatest blind spot, the radical left's greatest disaster, and the Jewish and Christian faiths' greatest glory.*

As stressed earlier, according to the Bible's view, we humans are created to be free and called to be free, but to be free we need to be *set free*—and delivery from the dark morass of hypocrisies, evils, injustices, and egregious abuses America has become mired in is an essential part of what America needs to be freed from. Indeed, America must face up to its desperate need for Isaiah Berlin's "negative freedom"—liberation from the burdens of the past just as the Israelites needed liberation from slavery under Pharaoh and John Bunyan's Pilgrim needed to have the burden removed from his back. But what is the Bible's way of liberation? The major steps can be set out simply and seen in terms of their implications for freedom.

First, truth must be addressed to power in confronting the evils, abuses, and hypocrisies. Under God there are three vital standards by which to assess and confront wrongs: the dignity and worth of humans made in the image and likeness of God, the objectivity of truth as the reality of reality, and the power of words both to create worlds and destroy worlds. Lies, abuse, and injustice violate any of these three standards. In America's case the evil of chattel slavery was that humans made in the image and likeness of their Creator degraded and abused their fellow humans who were also made in the image and likeness of their Creator. The hypocrisy of chattel slavery was that the same human beings used that created dignity to trumpet their liberty and equality while denying it to others. There must be no airbrushing of American history. To reject critical theory is not to deny the history it uncovers but to counter the endgame of revolution that it has in mind. Prophetic truth addressed to power is damning but liberating.

Second, there must be a call for repentance before God, for a turnabout of heart, mind, and spirit that acknowledges both the wrong done and the responsibility for any part in it. Repentance does not diminish the wrongs. The wrongs remain starkly and inexcusably wrong. They are seen as even more wrong because, through repentance, they are now acknowledged as wrong by both parties and not just the injured party. But a key part of the sting of the wrong would also be drawn. Repentance transforms the wrong significantly because in pronouncing the wrong to be wrong, the wrongdoers cancel their original intention and recast it as wrong. Both sides now see the wrong as wrong, and the wrongdoers now view the wrong in the same light as the wronged.

Thus, in repenting, the wrongdoers are making a commitment that if the same circumstances were to occur again, they would act differently the next time because they see things differently now. If the wrongdoers had known beforehand what they know now and had been able to feel beforehand what they feel now, they would not have done what they did. This of course covers the present as well as the future. It means that every remaining trace of American racism, whether in the present or the future, whether individual or institutional, must be confronted in the light of this decisive repentance. Repentance, too, is both damning and liberating.

Third, there must a voluntary admission and confession of the wrong—before the wronged or the family and descendants of the wronged if possible. Properly understood, voluntary confession is a rare moral act. Instead of excusing ourselves and rationalizing what happened as we humans usually do, wrongdoers who confess voluntarily *go on record against themselves*. Whenever someone says, "I wronged you" (or "I lied," "I cheated you," "I was rude to you," "I hurt you," "I abused you"), they are shouldering the personal responsibility for what they did and clearing the person who was wronged of any part in the wrong done to them. Confession is both damning and liberating.

Fourth, there can then be genuine forgiveness. True forgiveness (*forth-giving* or dismissing) is triply freeing. In freely forgiving the offense, the one who has been wronged, or who represents the wronged, chooses to break the downward spiral of action and reaction. Stopping it right there, there is no further accumulation, no carrying forward the burden of a grudge or resentment, and no further fueling of a cycle of violence, vengeance, and vendetta. (In Bunyan's seventeenth-century classic *Pilgrim's Progress,* he pictures forgiveness as the shedding of a burden on Pilgrim's back. In *The Power of Ideas*, Rabbi Sacks remarked somewhat more tongue-in-cheek that forgiveness is "the emotional equivalent of losing excess weight.") At the same time, when wrongdoers are forgiven the offense, they are freed from the burden and guilt of the past and freed for a future with a clean slate and a second chance. There is no burden looking back and no burden looking ahead. Forgiveness, as an act of freedom that frees even further, is truly liberating.

Fifth and finally, there can be reconciliation and restoration. The wrong that divided two people, or a family or a nation, is cleared away. Through genuine atonement enemies can become friends, and when truth and trust are restored, freedom can flourish once more. "Who is a hero?" the Jewish sages asked, knowing the traditional answer was

"One who defeats his enemies." Their answer was more powerful still, made possible by atonement. "Who is a hero? One who turns an enemy into a friend." Or as Lincoln once replied to a bystander, "Do I not destroy my enemies when I make them my friends?"

Stated so briefly, these five steps inevitably sound simple, if not simplistic. Yet there is nothing deeper, more profound, and more moving and transforming than the atonement of Yom Kippur as understood by Jews, and Good Friday as understood by Christians. The challenge of righting the world's wrongs demands of each of us personal and moral accountability that is a vital part of the examined life. The Jewish and Christian faiths are realistic, not utopian, about humanity. There must be no airbrushing of history and no rationalizing in our own lives either. Instead of "we/they" (with *we good* and *they bad*), the reality is always "we too." Self-righteousness can be as deadly as a blatant wrong. (Asked what was the problem with the world, G. K. Chesterton replied, "I am." Asked what he would do as the ruler of the world, Rabbi Sacks answered, "I would resign.")

The present generation has to confront the sins of the past, to which we are heirs, but we are as fallible as the past, so there must be no preening or virtue signaling. Before we judge others, we must judge ourselves and allow ourselves to be judged before the unbendable standards of God. In his *Ceremony and Celebration*, Rabbi Sacks writes profoundly of Yom Kippur what Christians believe of Good Friday too. These are the days that remind us of what is in all our hearts.

The distance between who we are and who we ought to be is, for most of us, vast. We fail. We fall. We give in to temptation. We drift into bad habits. We say or do things in anger we later deeply regret. We disappoint those who had faith in us. We betray those who trusted us. We lose friends. Sometimes our deepest relationships can fall apart. We experience frustration, shame, humiliation, remorse. We let others down. We let ourselves down. These things are not rare. They happen to all of us even the greatest.

ON WHAT GROUNDS?

Yet the realism and humbling of that admission is only the beginning of the story. There are two other essential parts too. Yom Kippur and Good Friday remind us of what is in all our hearts. But they do not leave us in despair because they offer forgiveness and atonement. God's forgiveness of us is the crucial part. Once we repent and are forgiven, it becomes possible to forgive others. Forgiven, we can forgive. Forgiven, we must forgive. And once we are forgiven, we can strive for an ethical life without fear of failure, to take our stand for justice in the world even though we know we are not perfect, and to confront the sins of the past without stumbling over our own hypocrisy.

All this is possible because Yom Kippur and Good Friday point us to the answer—God's free forgiveness for the wrong when we repent and confess to him. In other words, as we experience atonement and reconciliation with God ourselves, we can strive for atonement and reconciliation between others. "The problem of the world is me," but we can forgive because we have been forgiven, so we can be agents of reconciliation in our turn. We can become the change we would like to see in the world, without condescension and without self-righteousness, judgmentalism, hypocrisy, and overreaction. Without forgiveness, for example in the talk of reparations, each of these problems by itself becomes the ruin of justice and freedom, and when combined they spell disaster.

But there is a third part of the Bible's atonement too—the necessary basis. There has to be a costly solution to match the terrible cost of evil. The evil of human inhumanity to fellow humans is inexpressibly horrific, whether Cain murdering his brother Abel, Americans in their slavery, the British and the Belgians in their colonialism, the Germans and the Japanese in their death camps, the French in their revolutionary Reign of Terror, the Russians and Chinese in their extermination campaigns, or the many pyramids of skulls that stretch back through the centuries. And these are just examples of the monstrous and the well-known. What of the lies and abuses at the daily level in our families, our neighborhoods, our workplaces, and our politics? Is it all to be swept under carpet, the trivial and the monstrous? That way lies the road to accumulation and conflict and violence without end.

Is it any surprise that those who most appreciate the rottenness of their hearts, our hearts, and the utter vileness of the world's evils are the ones who know that no normal response will suffice? The blood still cries out from the ground, and it will not be silenced. There are evils that cry out to heaven and cry out for hell. (Hanging was "not enough," as people said after the trial of Adolf Eichmann.) To which the Bible agrees. The worse the evil, the greater must be the remedy. Is it any accident that those most outraged by the horrors of chattel slavery and the lynchings of the Jim Crow era are the loudest voices calling for justice as reparation in one form or another? With every fiber of their being they know that suffering people have paid a terrible price and somehow an equal price must be paid in return. To which the Bible agrees again, but it points to a judgment and a sacrifice more than equal to the evil it atones for. There is forgiveness for the vilest and the worst because of the sacrifice of the best. There is mercy for the least of us because of the death of the greatest. One who was innocent paid the price by giving up his life for the guilty that we might be forgiven and go free.

At the first Yom Kippur in the Sinai desert, there were two goats chosen to demonstrate Israel's atonement: one a sacrifice and the other a scapegoat. Following the crucifixion of Jesus as the supreme sacrifice on Good Friday, there has been a tendency to misuse the scapegoat—in other words to bypass the true sacrifice and its offer of forgiveness and a fresh start and to fasten on some poor person scapegoated to carry the pent-up hatred and violence of the people. America has already witnessed far too many assassinations of presidents such as Abraham Lincoln and John F. Kennedy, and national leaders such as Dr. Martin Luther King Jr. and Senator Robert Kennedy. The time has come to consider the only sacrifice powerful enough to deal with the mountainous guilt of the American past and the turbulent grievances and emotions of the present.

The unexamined heart and conscience are no more worth trusting than the unexamined life is worth living. Americans dare not sidestep the spiritual and moral requirements in facing and dealing with America's past. The Jewish and Christian understanding of Yom Kippur and Good Friday must not be dismissed as religious and irrelevant. Repentance, confession, forgiveness, reconciliation, and atonement are moral, spiritual, practical, and urgent. If what Jews call the human inclination toward evil and Christians call the propensity to sin is left unaddressed, the weight of America's guilt will bring the nation down in interminable conflicts. What Lincoln stated so clearly about the Civil War in his Second Inaugural Address is true today of America's conflicts over race.

Yet, if God wills that it continue until all the wealth piled by the bondsman's two hundred and fifty years of unrequited toil shall be sunk, and until every drop of blood drawn with the lash shall be paid by another drawn by the sword, as was said three thousand years ago, so still it must be said "the judgments of the Lord are true and righteous altogether."

Only the Bible's greatest glory can answer America's greatest evil. God forbid that America's evil should stay unaddressed, half-addressed, or wrongly addressed. Far better that some future day of (voluntary and nonofficial) national atonement will be the starting point for American renewal and a fresh flowering of freedom and justice. No other approach comes close to offering a remedy for America's egregious evils and abuses, but the obvious difficulties in considering it are what shape the challenge of the second question raised in the opening chapter.

Is it possible for America as the lead society of an immense civilization to examine its own conscience while at the height of its power, to make confession and amends for its evident wrongs—above all, for slavery and the treatment of the Native Americans—and to remedy, reform, and redirect its ways to the satisfaction of its citizens and the highest ideals of humanity? Or will America succumb to an orgy of politically organized recrimination and become the victim of its unforgiven past? If "We the people" still holds and there is enough of the politics of all Americans together, that is a question for American citizens and American leaders alike.

PASSING THE BATON

HANDING ON FREEDOM FROM
GENERATION TO GENERATION

THE BEIJING OLYMPICS in 2008 illustrated one of the central challenges facing American freedom. America has had relay runners on the winners' podium ever since relay races were first introduced to the Games, but in 2008 there were none. To be fair, Usain Bolt, "lightning Bolt," was peerless in the sprints that year and uncatchable in the next two Olympics, but that was not the reason for the absence of Americans. The truth was that again and again the American runners dropped the baton, and the watching millions around the world heard the hollow, tinny sound of the baton hitting the track. Relay races are won and lost in the smooth handing over of the baton, and the same is true of freedom. Freedom's last essential foundation stone to be put in place is transmission. If freedom is to endure, there must be a smooth and successful handing over of freedom from generation to generation.

The underlying challenge of transmission is simple. *If any project is to last longer than a single generation, it requires successful transmission, and successful transmission for a nation requires families, schools, and history.* Both faith and freedom share this imperative. They are never more than one generation away from extinction. Faith dies and freedom dies too if it is not handed on. Every generation is a pulse beat in the story of humanity, so a transmission's breakdown is like a heart attack in the life of a person or a dropping of the baton in a relay race.

THE GOLDEN TRIANGLE OF FREEDOM

This emphasis on transmission is a reminder of the major tasks involved in building and maintaining a free society—winning freedom, ordering freedom, and sustaining freedom. *Winning freedom* is the most obvious and glorious of the three. Freedom must be won through an uprising or revolution, often at great cost (as in the revolution of 1776). *Ordering freedom* is less obvious but equally important. Freedom requires a framework. It must be given a constitution and the political structures it can thrive within (as in the US Constitution of 1787). The third task, *sustaining freedom*, should be equally obvious, but it is the task that many people overlook. Not only does it take much longer—if freedom is to endure, it is the work of centuries rather than a few years—but it is also much harder (Benjamin Franklin's "A republic, Madame, if you can keep it"). I have argued in *A Free People's Suicide* that the American founders' views on sustaining freedom have been seriously neglected, but it is one of their most important and practical notions that is essential for freedom. The founders never gave their views a name, but we may call it "the golden triangle of freedom."

How did they propose that freedom was to be sustained? They repeatedly emphasized three vital principles that together form the legs of a triangle, which as they are linked become like the recycling triangle that goes around and around. First, freedom requires virtue. (Ben Franklin again: "Only a virtuous people are capable of freedom. As nations become more corrupt and vicious, they have more need of masters.") Second, virtue requires faith of some sort. Third, faith of any sort requires freedom. Thus, freedom is sustained when all three are working together—freedom requires virtue, which requires faith, which requires freedom, which requires virtue, which requires faith, which requires freedom—and so on ad infinitum. (The fuller explanation of each principle and their links are in my earlier book *A Free People's Suicide*.)

BEDROCK INSTITUTIONS

In America's case, transmission is carried along in many ways, including presidential inaugural addresses and farewell addresses. At their best these addresses rise to be America's equivalent of Israel's twin renewal ceremonies that were led by the king—one being a seven-year national rededication to the covenant and the other being a personal rededication as the king wrote out the covenant in his own hand and kept the scroll beside him as a reminder.

But the main burden of handing on freedom is carried by families and by schools. In covenantal-constitutional nations families are the bedrock of society, and to promote or tolerate the breakdown of the family is to disorder freedom at its core. Families mean love that generates new life; parenting means formation in identity, character, and the virtues from the earliest age, so that for better or worse families are the indispensable key to human identity, ethics, and civic continuity. If those ideas sound abstract, we should remember that the family accomplishes these things silently and unconsciously through such practical things as simply being together, conversations at the dinner table, bedtime stories, and the celebration of holidays.

Schools, in America's case public schools, are critical at a later age—especially through civic education, the teaching of what it is to be American and what citizenship of the American republic requires of each new generation of Americans.

All these things have gone by the board or have been disastrously weakened in America in the last generation. Families have become smaller and less stable. They have been broken by divorce and weakened by alternative forms of living together, parents have been sidelined by schools on one side and by video games and the social media on another, holidays have become casualties of the culture wars, and the family dining table has become a fast-food Grand Prix refueling station between sports games and other activities. Not only was civic education excised from public schools in the late sixties, but it was also replaced by Howard Zinn's alternative views of American history and then by the 1619 Project and radical views openly opposed to the American founding. Now, with President Biden allowing countless people to flood into the borderless south of the country, there is no civic education for the new arrivals and therefore no citizenship as classically understood and as required by freedom.

The combined result of such trends is suicidal for the American republic.

The earlier American motto *E pluribus unum* is now impossible. Without a solid understanding of citizenship for either the new arrivals or the rising generation, there is no *unum* to balance the *pluribus*. If rampant individualism spells chaos, immigration without citizenship spells the death of the republic as it was founded. In short, it is still relatively easy to enter America and become an American, but it is now harder and harder to know what it is to *be American*. The present generation has dropped the baton. America's transmission has broken down, and republican freedom will follow fast.

Here again the Jewish people are a study in contrast, and from Sinai on their successful transmission has been a secret of their incredible survival in the face of the most vicious prejudice, the most intense scattering, and the direst persecution. What did Moses talk about the night of the Passover? After more than four hundred years of slavery, they were going free. Yet remarkably, the rabbis point out, Moses did not mention freedom. Nor did he refer to the long-promised land, the land of milk and honey they were going to. Instead, three times Moses talked of children. The stories they were urged to tell their children would be the key to their identity and continuity as a people. God's new way, the Jewish project, his countercultural people, needed to be vigilant in keeping the transmission of their faith and their way of life both strong and healthy. Do Americans think they can relax in their prosperity and presume that the transmission of their own great experiment in freedom will be any less demanding?

CHECK THE FOUNDATIONS

America is a nation by intention and by ideas, and those ideas and ideals must be passed on without fail if freedom is to survive. The American economy may be powerful, and the American military is certainly formidable, but American greatness does not lie there. To make America great again lies in cultivating ideas and ideals, and that is where the torch of freedom must be kept burning brightly. But there are foundations for freedom too, and from the Bible's perspective three are essential above all.

First, freedom requires the foundation that every single person be viewed, valued, and treated in terms of their supreme dignity and worth. Created in the image and likeness of God, each human being is a unique person, precious, and unsubstitutable for any other. *Each individual human being carries this personhood and worth—regardless of color, creed, class, or culture.* The Genesis declaration of the *imago Dei* is color-blind, creed blind, class blind, and culture blind. Humanity as a life form created in the image of God is quite different from all other life forms on the earth, and therefore best understood upward, and not downward. Humans are individual persons in relation to God, before they are analyzed downward, either in terms of physical nature ("toolmakers," "naked apes," "selfish genes," and so on), in terms of their roles as citizens, voters, and consumers, or in terms of their problems and shortcomings (such as disabled, uneducated, and so on). Often, as the Jewish sages say, other people may not be in *my* image or *our* image, but every single person is in God's image, and we must therefore value and deal with them as such.

There is no greater assault on the sacredness of human dignity and ultimately on the entire human rights movement than the degradation of humanity in the pro-choice arguments for abortion. They flout not only the truth that human dignity is sacred and unsubstitutable but the plain and obvious truth that every single human life is unrepeatable. Once a life has been taken, there is no return. Had the US Supreme Court not passed *Roe v. Wade* in 1973, more than sixty million Americans would be with us today as family members, friends, and fellow citizens—in many parts of the world, they by themselves would constitute a good-sized nation, but they were not spared.

The futility and the perniciousness of critical theory and the antiracism movement are shown up at this point. They are the current expressions of identity politics. Like the Greek innkeeper Procrustes, they force people onto the bed of their categories and refuse to see people as anything other than members of groups—rich and poor, men and women, White and Black, straight and gay, oppressors and victims. Some people are therefore instantly and automatically condemned as members of a proscribed group ("All Whites are racists"), and others are instantly and automatically absolved ("Blacks are victims and therefore cannot be racists"). Identity politics has no place for the notion of human dignity, individual worth, and personal responsibility. Nor does it have any remedy for the evil it fights except shaming and assault.

Yet the truth is that created in the image of God all human beings are capable of both good and bad behavior—as individual persons and not simply as members of groups. Every single one of us is potentially a sinner and sinned against, a victim and a victimizer, and we must be judged as such by our actions. Thus, contrary to the dogmatic theories of victimization and intersectionality, sin is an equal-opportunity problem. Victims sin too. Victims of prejudice can be prejudiced too—and often are. There is no escape jail card for any of us. Thus, when critical theory and antiracism view people as only in groups, such as the Blacks and the powerless, and harps only on the sins and evils of others, such as the Whites and the powerful, they raise a double standard that condemns too many wrongly and clears too many wrongly. They also forget that sins and evils are never remedied by solely harping on sins and evils.

When we humans sin and do wrong, we require a remedy, but we also need a standard by which we can be restored as well as judged. Having neither a standard nor a remedy, identity politics can be only destructive, and antiracism can only condemn itself to become reverse racism. It refuses to see people as individual persons and, like the racist, insists on seeing them only in categories such as color, creed, class, and culture. The old racist may have seen a Black as inferior simply as a Black, whereas the reverse racist now sees a White as systemically evil simply as a White. But neither sees the individual person, and both are prejudiced. They make the same mistake. Antiracism mirrors and reinforces the racism it claims to fight, just as anticolonialism has become a new ideological colonizer. Both movements purport to pursue justice, but in turning a blind eye to individual personhood and focusing only on labels and stereotypes, the effect is to issue a license for expanding prejudice and inciting even further hate.

That is not to say that there is any moral equivalence between the old racism and the new. The old racism was unspeakably vile and wrong, but the new racism of the antiracist is no solution. American public life now demonstrates with stunning clarity that identity politics is a triple disaster. It dehumanizes people, divides society, and deepens the problem it sets out to solve.

Martin Luther King Jr.'s well-known position owed everything to his Christian faith and nothing to identity politics. What counts with people is the "content of their character," not the "color of their skin." Treating people as persons regardless of their color, creed, class, or culture is the beginning of justice as well as love in action. Justice is never purely legal. It is always personal and relational and not only public and institutional. It is a matter of how each person treats other persons with the same dignity and worth as themselves because they are made in the image of God, and how each person is treated by the courts and the institutions of society.

When individual human worth is abused, the result is inhumanity. But when individual human worth is respected as true and nonnegotiable, the reality of a human being is lifted into harmony with the ideal of being human. Genuine regard for personhood is where freedom, justice, and love become real and are best able to support each other in reality. Stress personhood above all else and there can be love and responsibility between people and throughout society, but stress categories of color, creed, class, or culture above personhood, and there will only be conflict and hate.

Second, freedom requires the foundation of a strong view of truth. The fatal error at the heart of postmodern thinking is its denial of truth, which means the eventual denial of freedom. If God is dead and there is no objective truth, all that remains is power. Yet power alone has always been the greatest menace to human freedom and the single greatest source of human abuse down the centuries. When power is all-decisive, victory goes to the strong, and the weak go to the wall. The powerful do what they want, and the weak do what they have to. Justice is perverted as the interests of the wealthy and the powerful, and viral shaming and public show trials are the fate of dissidents and dissenters who have no power.

Truth serves freedom by countering power in two ways, negatively and positively. First, truth counters power by promoting the *freedom from* of freedom. Truth highlights the falseness of all the powers that constrain our freedom wrongly. Truth exposes them as that which is wrong and that which should be otherwise—whether the false power derives its strength from alcohol, drugs, abusive relationships, an overbearing boss, an all-seeing high-tech media company, or a monstrous political tyranny such as Soviet Russia, Nazi Germany, or communist China.

Second, truth goes on to promote the *freedom for* of freedom. It highlights the truth of who we are and the truth of what we are capable of becoming. The positive role of truth is indispensable to both our freedom and our fulfillment.

Without truth we simply cannot be who we are or grow to be who we are capable of becoming. This double action of both the negative and the positive aspects of truth was the setting behind the famous words of Jesus: "You will know the truth and the truth will make you free" (John 8:32).

In our highly diverse world the importance of truth and the costs of untruth differ from country to country, from worldview to worldview, and from civilization to civilization. Contrast, as ever, is the mother of clarity. Western postmodernism prides itself naively and disastrously on its post-truth conclusions. Further east, both Hindus and Buddhists believe that what we think is reality is *maya* or illusion and impermanence. Further back, many Greeks and Romans held that truth was real and important but forever out of human reach. (Democritus: "Of truth we know nothing, for truth is in a well"; Cicero: "Nature has buried truth at the bottom of the sea.") In strong contrast to all these views, Jews and Christians hold that truth is all-important, ultimate, and undeniable because it is rooted in God who is true. Truth therefore matters supremely as "the reality of reality" or reality as it is before God.

To be sure, our God-given freedom means that we can shape reality to some extent according to what we wish it to be, at least in our thoughts and our words. But there is always a limit to falsehood, as the gender revolution is beginning to discover. Only truth is finally and fully aligned with reality, so people who stray from the truth court unreality, needless conflict, folly, and even greater dysphoria and misery. To be sure, there are no limits to human thinking, but thinking and saying something does not make it so. All ideas are thinkable, but not all ideas are livable. This means that truth is never purely theoretical and philosophical, and a lie is always more than a verbal discrepancy.

Whoever would live free must embrace the challenge of truth and truthfulness. We must pursue the truth steadfastly and unflinchingly not only in our thinking but in our living. Truth and truthfulness are not only the royal road to freedom but also the only road to freedom as well as to goodness, justice, health, and peace. Mendacity is the ruin of freedom, and America's culture of lies, hype, and spin is sounding the death knell of America's great experiment in freedom. To live freely under our own vine and fig tree requires people who prize the truth, who pursue the truth, who seek to know the truth, and to live in truth—citizens who are people of truth and enemies not only of the Big Lie but of all lies, falsehood, and unreality. Without truth, there cannot be and never in a million years will there be freedom.

Third, freedom requires the foundation of healthy respect for words. In America today words have been cheapened and hollowed out by adspeak, weaponized by politics, and poisoned by social media. The contrast of the high view of words in the Hebrew and Christian Scriptures offers a timely antidote. The very universe was created by a word, and the Creator of all there is, who cannot be captured in images, communicates in words. Words are therefore powerful and to be respected. Words create worlds, and words can destroy worlds. Our words are commitments. Our yes must be yes, our no must be no, and our word must be our bond.

Lies as the intention to deceive are a violation of truth as God knows it. Insults and demeaning speech, never clearer than in the atrocious tweets of former-President Trump, are a violation of the respect owed to a fellow human being created in the image of God. Promises that are made to dupe rather than deliver are a travesty of trust. Strikingly, the Jewish sages even regarded evil speech as tantamount to murder. It kills three people, not just one: the person it is said of, the person who says it, and the person who listens to it.

Evil speech that has no respect for either truth or personhood is a cancer on the truth and trust that make for a free society, and it quickly metastasizes into suspicion, hate, and violence. No president, no member of Congress, and no leader of any political party who tells brazen lies and indulges in abusive insults, as many of these leaders have recently, can pass themselves off as a champion of freedom. Fact checkers will certainly check, and liars will be awarded Pinocchios at times, but the problem is deeper than that. The seriousness lies in the fact that words matter to freedom. If freedom is to be sustained, our words must serve the high dignity of our humanness and the robust demands of truth and truthfulness. If America as the land of the free needs renewal and reformation at any point, it is without any question over Americans' use of words. "Free the word" is the watchword for regaining freedom more widely.

CELEBRATE HISTORY

Another key notion is the celebration of history. The Bible is also a study in contrast over history. Our human genius is to range backward through memory and forward through vision and imagination. Loss of history is therefore as damaging for a nation as Alzheimer's is for an individual. Thus, whereas the nations surrounding Israel celebrated festivals that were tied to nature and the cycle of the seasons, the Jewish festivals were celebrations of history and God's great actions on their behalf. Celebrated annually with fervor, the Jewish festivals were vital to the transmission of Judaism, for each succeeding generation entered into their history *as if they were there themselves*—at the Passover, at the giving of the covenant at Mount Sinai, at the forgiveness after the scandal of the golden calf, in crossing the wilderness in tents, and so on.

Needless to say, history is always explored and understood within a framework, and America must choose whether that framework is to be the founders' vision of republican freedom or the vision of today's radical left courtesy of Howard Zinn and the 1619 Project. The choice is crucial. These two visions cancel each other out, so there must be no airbrushing of either view or any facile attempt to pretend they can be harmonized. History is essential for the republican view of freedom. It serves as an aid to strengthen human promise-keeping and its importance for the covenant. Left to ourselves we humans easily forget the past, we do not know the future, and we are often fickle in the present. Nothing lasts forever, no one stays young forever, and nothing remains fresh forever. Time and death are therefore the constant enemies of freedom, and the repeated call to "Remember" and "Not forget" are bracing and necessary. This is especially so in times of power and prosperity when all is secure and the temptation to complacency is strong.

Strikingly, the Bible underscores this general admonition in a special way for leaders. The Hebrew king was commanded to be humble and "that his heart may not be lifted up above his countrymen" (Deuteronomy 17:19-20). "Mr. President, it's not about you." But the king was also commanded to study the covenant constantly *while he was king*. The king was commanded to read the covenant "all the days of his life" (Deuteronomy 17:19). "Mr. President, upholding the Constitution goes beyond your swearing-in. You have counselors, advisers, assistants, press secretaries, and entire departments and armies at your command, but you cannot delegate the leadership of a free republic. Like the great Jewish leader Moses or like Winston Churchill with his immense grasp of history, your task is to guide the destiny of the American republic with a profound and ever-growing understanding of the ideas and ideals of the American republic and the best and worst of the American past. To 'make America great again,' Mr. Trump, and to 'restore the soul of America,' Mr. Biden, you must address what made America America in the first place."

In his Second Inaugural Address in 1985, President Reagan spoke of America's calling to work for the "triumph of human freedom under God." Transmission is essential to freedom and to such a mission statement, and so also is rededication and renewal—both the national renewal of the Declaration and Constitution and the personal renewal of individual citizens. America appears to have forgotten both its mission and the requirements of freedom. Following the way of freedom means respecting what freedom requires generation after generation without fail, always remembering the past and its celebrations and its warnings. There is simply no other way to be free, to remain free, to renew freedom, and to stay the hand of the otherwise inevitable decline and fall of great nations. To forget the inspiration and warning of the past is to starve and suffocate freedom and court decline. Only in remembering and celebrating the past can freedom flourish, and only in handing it on and renewing it when necessary can you love your children and your children's children as yourselves.

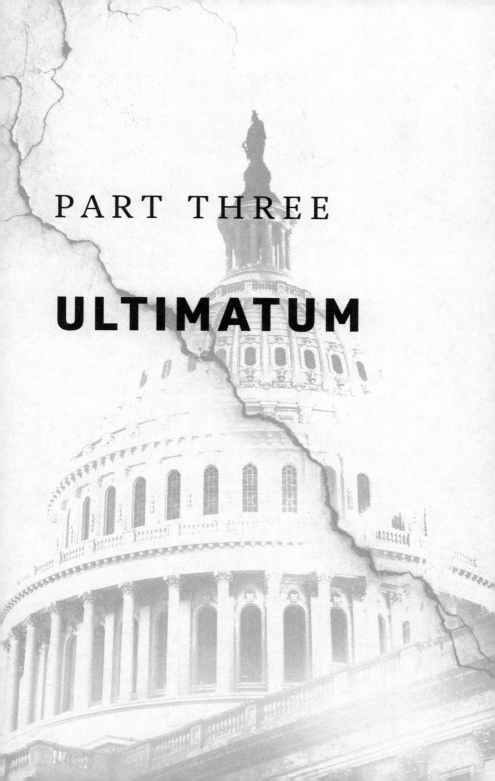

PART THREE

ULTIMATUM

ZERO HOUR AMERICA

THE INVISIBLE HAND is writing on the wall, and letter by letter and word by word the full sentence is growing clearer and easier to read. "Weighed in the balance and found wanting." Americans now face their Belshazzar moment, which will be decisive for them as citizens and for the standing of the American republic in the world today—and for America's place in history. Like the people of any nation there are basic questions that Americans must always ask themselves. Who are you? Where have you come from? Where are you now? Where are you going? And to whom or what do you hold yourselves accountable? (To yourselves, to your founding, to history, to universal ideals, or to God?) Such questions are foundational and enduring, and they require historical wisdom, visionary imagination, and moral awareness that are the hallmark of great nations and great leaders. In recent years serious answers to such basic questions have been conspicuously absent in America's presidents and political leaders, with rare exceptions such as President Reagan and the occasional flourishes of presidential speechwriters. This deficiency in basic American leadership has become so striking that the dearth of national leadership is now a serious part of the overall American crisis in itself.

What are the chances of America reexamining the character and requirements of freedom, redirecting its course, including a fresh consideration of Washington's vision of citizens living free under their own vine and fig tree? To many Americans the very mention of freedom has become a cliché, and Washington's vision sounds quixotic. But more importantly the foundational ideas for the first president's vision come from a source other than the one Americans are currently quarrying. For some time now America has been exploring freedom further and further from its roots, and many of the nation's thinkers are running pell-mell down alternative paths, not realizing they are the wrong paths and they lead to the rocks.

Recent events—from bitterly disputed elections to controversial responses to the global pandemic, to the humanitarian and civic crisis on the southern border, to domestic threats to free speech, to crippling national debt, to the American humiliation in Afghanistan, to the emergence of an intelligentsia at odds with the nation's founding ideals, to growing authoritarian attitudes and actions, to troubling questions about presidential character and stability—are shaking Americans awake, and a long-overdue assessment of the state of the Union must begin. Let me repeat the titanic questions that the American republic and its citizens now face, the answers to which will prove decisive for the future of America.

First, is it wise and is it possible for Americans to switch revolutions in midcourse in history—from the ideals of 1776 to the ideals of 1789? And if not, is it possible for the present heirs of history's greatest experiment in ordered freedom to remember and restore the promise of their original revolution, with a firm but humble conviction of its distinctiveness in relation to other ways of arranging societies and nations? Or will America hasten its downfall through vacillating between the legacy of the two revolutions and harvesting the bitter fruits of uncertain and contentious views of freedom, justice, and community?

Second, is it possible for America as the lead society of an immense civilization to examine its own conscience while at the height of its power, to make confession and amends for its evident wrongs, and to remedy, reform, and redirect its ways to the satisfaction of its citizens and the highest ideals of humanity?

Third, will Americans recognize the character of freedom and respond to freedom as freedom itself requires, or will they continue to follow faulty and specious views of freedom and remain satisfied with their distortions and imitations until they suffer irreversible decline? Not all who cry freedom have the grounds for the freedom they cry out for, and many of their views sound the death knell, not the Liberty Bell, for freedom, but can Americans any longer tell the difference?

Fourth, does America have leaders with sufficient wisdom, courage, sense of history, and an understanding of the character of freedom to guide the American people in considering and answering these questions and to do so in such a constructive way that they bring together a deeply divided people and reinvigorate a sense of united American identity and national purpose?

These are watershed questions and history and humanity wait for America's answer. The difference between the options in each case could hardly be starker and more consequential. Is America facing up to these questions? Is America intellectually and morally capable of doing so? Unless this happens, the "Howl, America!" that echoes the lament of the Hebrew prophets and the Beat poet may soon be followed by the "O America, America" that echoes the sorrowful lament of Jesus of Nazareth over Jerusalem, "O Jerusalem, Jerusalem" (Luke 13:34). In Shakespeare's words in *Julius Caesar*, "There is a tide in the affairs of men, which taken at the flood, leads on to fortune." And there are tides that, missed for one reason or another, leave people in the shallows or pull them down to shipwreck. The difference lies in the willingness to recognize, or fail to recognize, the meaning of the "full sea"—the character of the generation, the day, the hour, and the moment we are living in. America is at a moment that Americans dare not miss.

MASTERS OF HISTORY

Behind this challenge of discerning the times are other questions, and above all the question of different attitudes to time, history, and progress. Can we humans conquer time, or will time conquer us? Are we the masters of history or the dupes and pawns of history, or is there a better way between these two extremes? Is progress to be understood as a steady and successful upward climb, as the Enlightenment claimed? Hindus and Buddhists believe in a cyclical view of time, which has never offered either a high view of the arena of history or of human action. Life is lived in *maya,* or illusion. Jews and Christians, on the other hand, believe in a covenantal view of time. History under God is providential, and human action is crucial. Life is essentially historical, and history has purpose.

In contrast to both these views of life and the world, most modern secularists have a purely chronological view of time. There is no ultimate meaning in history. Behind events there is only a blank, but blank meaninglessness is unlivable. The pressure, then, is on humans to impose their own meaning on history. Either humans prove they are the masters of history, stamping their meaning and achievements on the face of time, or the final absurdity of human accomplishments stares them in the face. Regardless of these philosophical considerations, there is no question that in America's present crisis the masters-of-history attitude is alive and well, and it makes for confidence bordering on complacency, myopia, and delusion.

Yes, of course there are problems, many Americans say, even grave problems. But if we can put a man on the moon and explore the far reaches of space, we can solve our problems here if we only decide to do so and put our heads together. The best is yet to be. The nation that recovered from the Civil War and bounced back from the depression era can brace itself again and rise to face today's challenges too. The pendulum swings, but it swings back. The cycles may look extreme, but they return to where they began. Even in the worst-case scenario America will muddle through somehow. With the spirit of human nature's "hope springs eternal," combined with the do-it-yourself confidence of Enlightenment progress, Americans can start all over again—and if need be, again and yet again. America's best is yet to be, as the politicians repeat endlessly. There is no end to the resets that can be announced as they set out to promote their agendas.

To be sure, this starting-all-over confidence is nourished by the same spirit as the optimism of a New Year's resolution and often lasts only a little longer. It is amply boosted, of course, by America's self-help industry, with its cornucopia of ads, gurus, and products. America has become the Oprah wonderland of the "road map revolutions," where promise and possibility look their brightest and habits and routines seem their weakest and easiest to overcome. In the great American self-help world, road maps toward change are always in the air, the old way is never the only way, smiling prophets of human potential are offering new wares around the clock, and a thousand novel recipes for complete and final transformation can be ours for a click or two. This time, people are told each time, their health, their faces, their bodies, their bank balances, their lives, their worlds, and their futures can all be made anew—or at least until the next "new and improved" offer arrives and brings them even closer to the promise of the golden dawn that tomorrow promises.

In truth, this powerful sense of creating the world anew, starting all over, and reset is only writ small in New Year resolutions and self-help consumerism. It is magnified and writ infinitely larger in the grand hinge moments of history, such as in revolutions and in the boldest mass movements in the modern world.

The French revolutionaries declared that the day that Louis XVI was deposed (September 21 1792), was to be Day One in their Year One at the inauguration of their new calendar. (The new arrangement lasted until 1806 when the Gregorian calendar was reintroduced.)

In the Russian Revolution the Bolsheviks announced that all the Soviet Union must stop for five full minutes at 4 p.m. on January 21, 1924, the moment Comrade Lenin had died. "Time had stopped," the state radio intoned. The great leader was to be embalmed for the ages. They were embarked on a great immortality project like that of Ramses II and the pharaohs, and "Lenin's body should last forever," to be visited by his grateful people in his grand mausoleum in Red Square for all time.

In Italy in 1909, F. T. Marinetti launched his "Manifesto of Futurism." He boldly announced that

> we are on the extreme promontory of the centuries! What is the use of looking behind at the moment when we must open the mysterious shutters of the impossible? Time and Space died yesterday. We already live in the absolute because we have created eternal and omnipresent speed. . . . It is in Italy that we are issuing this manifesto of ruinous and incendiary violence, by which we today are founding Futurism, because we want to deliver Italy from its gangrene of professors, archaeologists, tourist guides and antiquarians.

Midnight on Tuesday, May 8, 1945, was the moment Germany declared to be its *stunde null*, or "zero hour." Hitler had died. The thousand-year Reich was over, an entirely new and democratic nation was born, and Germans were starting all over again.

In January 2021, Klaus Schwab and Prince Charles announced to the World Economic Forum in Davos, Switzerland, that the "Fourth Industrial Revolution" was underway, and it was time for a "Great Reset" of global capitalism to lead the world forward after the coronavirus pandemic of 2020. Emerging from Covid-19 represents "a rare but narrow window of opportunity to reflect, re-imagine, and reset our world."

In each of these cases, though in different ways, the promise was that the world could be made anew. Like revolutions, zero hours are relative, and we have to ask who says so and why. The zero hours of the Paris Jacobins and the Moscow Bolsheviks are quite different from the zero hours of the German democrats and the Davos capitalists. Then too there are greater and lesser zero hours—for two millennia the greatest divide in history has been the birthday of Jesus of Nazareth, giving us history's division between BC and AD. Even within the different zero hours, there are differences over the weight that each one puts on the old and the new. With revolutions the accent is always on the new. A new day has dawned and the long nightmare of the ancient régime is past and gone. At other times, the accent is on the old. The revolutionary *new*, whatever it was, is now considered neither as revolutionary nor as welcome as previously thought, and the older *old* is not as bad as people once believed. There are times when it is wise to go back to go forward, and the new is the old restored and reformed.

What counts, however, in all these claims is confidence in human mastery—in seeing the moment, seizing the opportunity, and resetting the expectations. Call the attitude rationalism, secularism, progressivism, technicism, elitism, utopianism, or view the mastery as the crowning combination of them all. What matters, we are told, is that we can trust those in charge to rise to the challenge of the present hour. There is certainly a crisis in America, the masters of history affirm, but it is no more than a routine crisis, and routine problems have routine solutions. You need only find the requisite pundit/consultant/expert/manager and the outcome is assured. The best and brightest are there to bail us out. With the "wizardry of the wise" all will soon be well again. "Progress" has lost all pretensions of being moral. Today it is technologically driven. Will not the iPhone 20 be superior by definition to the iPhone 19 when it arrives?

MONITORS OF THE CYCLES

At the opposite extreme from the *masters of history* are the *monitors of the cycles*—those who believe in clear patterns and discernible rhythms and cycles in the rise and fall of nations and civilizations in history. Many of the greatest exponents have an unassailable stature in their fields. Arnold Toynbee's twelve-volume *A Study of History*, for example, extended to more than three million words. It stands as the largest work of history ever and the longest book in the twentieth century. Yet for all the eminence of the best historians, the present temptation is that, as the Western and the American crisis deepens, people resort to these cycles and use their explanations from the past to find comfort in the turbulence and to make predictions for today. There are, of course, patterns, rhythms, and cycles in life and nature: spring, summer, autumn, winter, and our own birth, growth, maturity, and death as individual human beings. For Plato and Aristotle that meant simply that no political regime, whether a monarchy, an aristocracy, or a democracy, is ever stable and lasting. Each has a corrupt form as well as an ideal form, with monarchy degenerating into tyranny, aristocracy into oligarchy, and democracy into mob rule. But the wheel turns constantly, and there is no exact science in the constant turning of the wheel. History is messier than that.

Many historians and sociologists go further. They trace the grand patterns of history and some even claim to know the science of the cycles. They believe they have discovered the key formula at stake, and with this formula they can chart the rise and fall of nations and empires with considerable precision. The most famous of these historians include Sima Qian (in the second-century BC in China), Ibn Khaldun (at Al Azhar in fourteenth-century Cairo), Giambattista Vico (in eighteenth-century Italy), Oswald Spengler (with his *Decline of the West* in Germany after the First World War), Arnold Toynbee and John Glubb (both in twentieth-century England), and Pitirim Sorokin (born and raised in Russia but living and working in the United States as the founder of the sociology department at Harvard). And Philip Rieff (with his notions of "first worlds" based on fate, "second worlds" based on faith, and "third worlds" based on fiction).

There are major differences between the theories. Spengler, for example, was the "master doomsayer" of the modern world. His *Decline of the West,* or more literally his

Going Under of the Evening Lands, was deterministic and pessimistic, whereas Toynbee, Sorokin, and Rieff were even greater scholars, but they were open-ended and not deterministic. (Toynbee: "We cannot say for certain that our doom is at hand; and yet we have no warrant for assuming that it is not.") Renewal was always possible, Toynbee and Sorokin believed, though it only delayed but could not reverse the overall course of history. Or again, the lifespan of the Chinese powers is almost twice the length of the Arab powers simply because the Chinese dynasties that Sima Qian observed moved more slowly and lasted longer on average than the Islamic dynasties that Ibn Khaldun observed.

These historians' and social scientists' observations about history are highly enlightening. For Sima Qian and the Chinese the determining principle was moral—a crisis of the Mandate of Heaven—whereas for Ibn Khaldun, the determining principle was social: *asabiyya* or a crisis of the social solidarity and esprit de corps of the people. (Ibn Khaldun's understanding of the seeds of a nation's destruction are very similar to James Bryce's analysis of the "completest revolution" mentioned in chapter four and Emile Durkheim's notion of "anomie," the disorder, despair, and suicides that result from the breakdown of a nation's social cohesion.) More recently Philip Rieff's analysis of "culture creation" and "culture conflict" throws more light on America's culture wars than almost any other analyst writing today.

Cynics quip that if America and the West decline as these writers have outlined, no nation and no civilization will have had the benefit of reading their own obituaries so clearly, so often, and at such length. But to their credit the great strength of these thinkers and the enduring appeal of their theories is that they take history seriously and take in far more of history than most specialist historians. Many modern people, and especially the younger generation, stand indicted by Friedrich Hegel's famous charge in his *Lectures on the Philosophy of History*: "What experience and history teaches us is this—that people and governments have never learned anything from history, or acted upon any lessons they might have drawn from it." History underscores that nothing lasts forever, and each society contains the seeds of its own destruction. History is invaluable and indispensable to an examined life and to a wise leader.

At the same time, there is a weakness in some of these theories that carries over to their advocates today—the underlying determinism of the theories and the sense of fate and pessimism that some of them convey, supremely Spengler. If the mastery of history tends to appeal to the optimists, the monitoring of the cycles appeals mostly to the pessimists. Yet the truth is that the future is never strictly determined by the past, and the one thing we do not know and will never know is what tomorrow will bring. Human freedom and not fate, liberty and neither chance nor necessity are what decide the course of history and the future of societies and nations. Renewal is as possible as decline. This clear insistence on human freedom and responsibility, along with providence, is what distinguishes the Bible's view from both the masters of history on one side and the monitors of the cycles on the other.

Sir John Glubb may be right that the average age of a nation or an empire's greatness is 250 years, but that need not mean that America's greatness will be over on July 4, 2026. The American republic can rise, flourish, decline, and fall or be renewed to flourish and endure, all according to the principles of its founding and the choices it continues to make in the light of its founding and its character. That is why the seven foundation stones of freedom, covered earlier, are so important. Freedom rises and falls, flourishes or declines, endures, collapses, or is renewed according to the character and dynamics of freedom—and that is what Americans must remember and cannot afford to forget. The land of the free must show that it understands and respects the character of freedom. False freedoms fail and always will. Only true freedom lasts, but true freedom makes moral demands, and lasting freedom is a moral achievement, not a given or a right.

There are numerous differences between the many voices describing the decline of the West. But there is almost unanimity on one point. Barbarians, enemies, and other external pressures play their part in the decline, as was obvious with the famous sack of Rome by Alaric in AD 410. But the core reason for the decline is always internal. Nations and civilizations, just as with America now, rise and fall according to forces that are internal and not external. Russia, China, Iran, and North Korea currently pose the greatest challenge to America, but America is bringing America down. History underscores, and Americans should ponder again, what the twenty-eight-year-old Abraham Lincoln stated simply: "If destruction be our lot, we must ourselves be its author and finisher. As a nation of freemen, we must live through all time, or die by suicide."

Skeptics should contemplate the contrast between and the fate of the world's great empires and the near-miraculous survival of the Jewish people over four millennia, despite the viciousness of anti-Semitism and the most intense persecution and scattering of the Jews. Where are the empires of the Babylonians, the Egyptians, the Assyrians, the Persians, the Greeks, the Romans, the Aztecs, the Incas, the Spanish, the Dutch, and the British? They have run their course according to the run and rules of history, and so too will America and its empire if Americans ignore the character of freedom and responsibility and the requirements of each. Should Americans choose wisely and live well, renouncing the dangers and follies of freedom's look-alikes, renewal and flourishing are as possible as decline. If they fail to do so, their verdict can only be self-chosen. That is why it is imperative for Americans to understand and respect the character and dynamics of freedom, to know what they must do if its transmission and renewal are to be successful, and therefore to know how to choose wisely today.

THE CHOICE BEFORE AMERICA

We are therefore back again to the foundational issue of this essay. *Choose, America, choose, and choose as the character of freedom requires.* With the roots of America's ordered freedom in the Hebrew and Christian Bible, and the Bible's foundational insistence on human freedom and responsibility, the American republic must attend to the dynamics and requirements of freedom and responsibility if the republic is to endure. The alternative is for America to stand or fall according to the predictable cycles and lifespans of other nations and empires in history. Just as Alfred Nobel famously read his own obituary and changed the course of the rest of his life, including establishing his Peace Prize, so America and the West at large can read its own obituary in the grand works of historians such as Toynbee and Sorokin and respond accordingly. The *kairos* moment facing America can therefore be summed up as a series of choices Americans must make in light of the freedom that has made America. The following seven issues are paramount.

First, America must decide what freedom is, what freedom requires, what it means to be "the land of the free," and whether Americans wish to retain that identity after two and a half centuries. What is freedom? How is its ordered freedom to be understood? Is the nation first and foremost a republic or a democracy? What do these two notions mean in the light of freedom? How are they to be related, and how are they different from similar republics and democracies earlier in history and elsewhere in the world? When all America's diverse historical influences and factors are examined and weighed, is there any question that the chief roots of the American Revolution and the American republic are found in the Hebrew Scriptures and in what the seventeenth century called "the Hebrew republic"? Or that their principal source was the influence of the Reformation and that along with freedom the leading notions were such biblical themes as human dignity, justice, peace, covenant, community, the consent of the governed, and the separation of powers?

Americans are of course free to reject these roots and these principles. An overwhelming number of America's intelligentsia have already done so. Freedom truly is freedom. But precisely because freedom is freedom, and it flourishes in certain ways and declines and dies in other ways, it needs to be understood and respected to be sustained. Yet the present generation is strikingly careless about freedom, about the first principles of America's covenantal-constitutional order, and about the collective responsibility of a free people. Whether America chooses to retain its founding identity or not, that choice should be made in the clear light of how freedom was understood and what America's identity has been. What *The Federalist Papers* did for the Constitutional Convention, a fresh and powerful restatement of the founding character of America needs to do for our time.

Second, America must decide whether it wishes to continue to be a covenantal-constitutional republic as it was founded after the American Revolution or whether Americans choose to reconfigure their understanding of freedom and its identity and character along the line of ideas that have come from the French Revolution. There is a world of difference between these two revolutions and these two sources, and it would be a fateful error to slide across from one revolution to the other without careful thought and a solemn decision.

It is a stunning but lamentable fact that many Americans have no idea that commonly accepted ideas and movements such as *postmodernism, identity politics, tribal politics, radical multiculturalism, the sexual revolution, critical theory, political correctness, and the cancel culture* owe nothing to 1776 and everything to 1789. America is so far down the path of ideas from the French Revolution that only courageous leadership, a robust national debate, and a momentous national decision can hope to bring the nation back. And if America does choose to go back to the ideas and ideals of its own revolution, there will need to be a solemn and deliberate national renewal of the American covenant (on some future Fourth of July on the National Mall?), as well as a comprehensive restoration of civic education in America's public schools.

Third, America as the lead society in the Western world must take the lead in articulating and building a vision of society that is the constructive response to three revolutionary alternatives to Western civilization. Each is like a separate lava flow that has poured out from the volcanic explosion of the French Revolution: *revolutionary nationalism*, from Napoleon in nineteenth-century France to Carl Schmitt in 1930s Germany to Xi Jinping in twenty-first-century China; *revolutionary socialism* or communism, from Karl Marx and Friedrich Engels to modern China, Cuba, North Korea, and Venezuela; and *revolutionary liberationism,* from critical theory to transgender studies in the different forms of the neo-Marxism or cultural Marxism that has come down from thinkers such as Antonio Gramsci, Herbert Marcuse, and Michel Foucault. Through its blindness toward these dangers, especially now the third, the West is gambling the civilization that created it and hastening its own end.

Fourth, America must summon its strength to defend itself against three implacably hostile forces that are openly opposed to Western civilization and to the American republic: the *red wave*, representing the spectrum of Marxist and radical socialist alternatives to the ideals of representative government; the *black wave*, representing the post-1979 expressions of radical Islamism, such as Al-Qaeda, Hamas, Hezbollah, ISIS, Boko Haram, Al-Shabab, and the Taliban; and the *rainbow wave*, representing the radical wings of the sexual revolution whose architects, such as Wilhelm Reich, have openly stated that they intend to undermine three thousand years of Western civilization, including institutions such as the family and the church.

Fifth, as stated in chapter four, America must wake up and safeguard itself against three powerful trends that have combined to form the cultural climate change that is no less damaging to the American republic and Western civilization than climate change: *philosophical cynicism, moral corruption*, and *social collapse*. The effect of the fraying, social erosion, and unraveling caused by these trends is the modern variant of the crisis of social solidarity and esprit de corps identified by Ibn Khaldun in the fourteenth century as the principal cause of the collapse of nations.

Sixth, as stated in chapter three, America must debate and decide between the straightforward choices it now faces: *Revolution* (following the late sixties' "Long march through the institutions" and the inroads of cultural Marxism into America's colleges and universities, the press and the media, and Hollywood and entertainment); *Oligarchy* (following the hollowing out of traditional American liberalism and the consolidation of politics, bureaucracy, intelligence services, journalism, academia, and now business to create the menace of one-party national politics); and *Homecoming* (in the Hebrew sense that a decisive change of mind and heart is also a return and a homecoming).

Seventh, Americans must now survey their own history, examine both their individual consciences as well as their national conscience, and choose between the two main ways to address the array of wrongs, evils, and hypocrisies, such as racism and slavery, which they acknowledge: Can there be peace in the city? Can there be healing for the fractured republic? Is the remedy the way of the Bible or the way of the revolutionary left? There is an ocean of differences between these two approaches, and the difference in outcomes would not only be vast but final. The way of the Bible addresses truth to power and calls for repentance, confession, forgiveness, reconciliation, and restoration—putting wrongs right and transforming enemies into friends. The way of the revolutionary left is to weaponize victims and wage a merciless conflict of power against the status quo. There always has been and can only be one outcome to the second approach—what the Romans called "the peace of despotism," the state of affairs where an unrivaled power has sufficient power to silence and suppress all other powers. In a word, authoritarianism or Caesarism, which under the conditions of modernity means totalitarianism.

A WARNING IS NOT A PREDICTION

I have stated these seven challenges baldly. They require far deeper consideration and debate. But as Americans consider these choices and make their decision, they should keep in mind two final reminders. First, *freedom means that this essay is a warning and not a prediction.* To be sure, I have written strongly: for example, that "America will fall—unless." Some people will read that sentence alone and sidestep the challenge by accusing me of that most un-American sin, being a pessimist—even as they rest their confidence on an optimism built on sand. But in fact they would be wrong. I am not a pessimist. The American journey is not over, and it need not finish prematurely. I am fired by hope and the prospect of American renewal but with a clear-eyed realism that looks reality in the white of the eye. The root of the critics' error lies in confusing a warning with a prediction.

No people have a clearer understanding of the difference than the Jews, with the unique magnificence of their prophetic tradition. Rabbi Sacks states the crucial difference clearly in his *Studies in Spirituality*:

> Hence there is a fundamental difference between a prophecy and a prediction. *If a prediction comes true it has succeeded. If a prophecy comes true, it has failed.* A prophet delivers not a prediction but a warning. He or she does not simply say, "This will happen," but rather, "This will happen unless you change." The prophet speaks to human freedom, not to the inevitability of fate.

In short, even at this late stage in America's crisis freedom is still the issue. Nature may be strictly determined, but human nature is not. We humans need never be simply objects, whether to the worst of dictators seeking to oppress us or to the best of scientists seeking to understand us. Freedom means that we always can be subjects and agents. The possibility of repentance and its about-face of heart, mind, and spirit (in Hebrew *teshuvah* and in Greek *metanoia*) means that we are never reducible to the sum of the forces and factors constraining us at any particular moment. Created in the image of God, we are human, and we are free to change our minds. Repentance means that the future is open for a choice through which we can genuinely turn around and go in a different direction.

The possibility of forgiveness goes even further than repentance in its promise of freedom. The radical left harps on the sins of America's past, but like the revolutions that are its matrix, the radical left is ruthless. There is no shred of mercy or forgiveness in the speech codes, the cancel culture, the shaming, and the statue toppling. The rush to the guillotine is relentless and unstoppable. Once accused, the guilty are indefensible. Thus, the prospects for America on offer from secularists and the radical left are dismal. Postmodernism denies truth, naturalism denies freedom, and neo-Marxism denies mercy. With no freedom in their view of human nature, only determinism, and no forgiveness over the American past, only an accumulation of guilt, the sole solutions left are either abasement before power or appeasement before the powerful—Caesarism and the peace of despotism again.

The Bible's way of freedom through forgiveness is quite different. There is truth, there is freedom, and there is mercy and forgiveness. Together, they transform the worst of situations. Instead of the dread trio—accumulation, abasement, and appeasement—there can be atonement and freedom through the decisive removal of guilt. Acting together, repentance and forgiveness transform the past, the present, and the future by removing the guilt and reframing time under God. Rabbi Sacks's conclusion in the same book is stunning. "We cannot change the past. But by changing the way we *think about* the past, we can change the future." Will America decline or be renewed, stand or fall? All will come down to the choice between the extremely bad news at the heart of 1789 and the radical left and the extremely good news behind the heart of 1776 that is in the Jewish and Christian faiths.

IF YOUR HEART TURNS AWAY

Second, *freedom means that the heart of freedom is the freedom of the heart.* Freedom, love, the patriotism that is a genuine love of one's country, and the sacrifice that such passions are willing to make, all begin in the heart and are destroyed in the heart. As Thomas Hobbes and Adam Smith both realized, there are aspects of liberal democracy and the market economy that appeal only to reason and self-interest, but reason and the calculation of self-interest are no substitute for the freedom and love that true patriotism requires. Freedom, love, and patriotism are only as strong as they are strong in the hearts and minds of each succeeding generation of citizens.

Religious freedom, or freedom of religion and conscience, has long been prized as America's first liberty. It protects the inner forum of the conscience, which parallels the outer forum of the civic public square. Political freedom in any country is safe and strong when freedom of conscience is well respected and well protected in both the inner and the outer forums of the country. But the freedom of the heart lies even deeper than freedom of conscience. The heart is where freedom begins and where the love of freedom must be cherished and sustained, but no law, regulation, statute, police force, or army can protect the freedom of the heart. Nuclear weapons are powerless before the human heart. High-tech surveillance now spies on more and more of life, but not the heart. The heart is why the cultivation, guardianship, and transmission of freedom must be constant and why families and schools matter supremely. It is also why the practice of America's Pledge of Allegiance is so important, and why the kneeling controversy is so deadly to America— and far deadlier than in countries with monarchs and dictatorships that have no pledge and do not depend on any freely chosen consent or promise-keeping.

To talk of the human heart sounds soft, but it is far more than red-heart emoji sentimentalism. The heart is the center and soul of a human being and of our being human. Out of the heart come our thoughts, our will, our decisions, and our actions. If we are to stand free and responsible in public life, we must start freely and responsibly in our personal lives and then live freely and responsibly through all our lives from our hearts outward. America tends to forget this alpha point and then oscillates between sentimentalism and legalism. Americans have narrowed constitutionalism to a matter of law and law courts, and the roots of the constitution in covenant-making have been obscured. But like a covenant, a constitution depends on freely chosen consent and a morally binding pledge, so a covenant is a promise from the heart before it is a signature on a page or an oath recited in public.

Many Americans have forgotten that *constitution* comes from *covenant* and that America's early expressions such as the Mayflower Compact, the Constitution of the Commonwealth of Massachusetts, and 1787's US Constitution and "We the people" owe everything to the precedent and pattern of the exodus covenant at Mount Sinai. Constitution for many Americans today is no more than articles, amendments, and appeals, Supreme Court decisions, and lawyers, lawyers, and more lawyers. Yet the best American lawyers have been those who remind America that the Constitution is far more than law. In 1931, Andrew Cunningham McLaughlin ended his magisterial *Foundations of American Constitutionalism* with a reminder of the need for "common beliefs and principles" that were deeper than the law. Thirteen years later, Judge Learned Hand spelled out the point unforgettably in his great wartime speech in Central Park, New York. "Liberty lies in the hearts of men and women; when it dies there, no constitution, no law, no court can save it; no constitution, no law, no court can do much to help it." Freedom, love, patriotism, and the renewal and destruction of them all begin in the heart.

America's present choice, then, cannot and will not be decided by congressional legislation, by a Supreme Court decision, or by the election of a president and the victory of any party. John Adams said the same thing of the revolution itself. "The Revolution was effected before the war commenced. The Revolution was in the hearts and minds of the people. . . . This radical change in the principles, opinions, sentiments, and affections of the people was the real Revolution." That is as true today as it was for Adams and as it was even earlier for the people of Israel at Mount Sinai. The consent and the promise of "We the people" begins and ends in the heart. If America's renewal and rededication are to be real today, the choice for renewal must be real in the hearts and minds of citizens from the northern border to the southern border, from coast to coast, and from the oldest to the youngest.

The choice before America today is like the choice Moses put before Israel in the last month of his long life. Israel is not America and America is not Israel, but because of their common roots there are crucial similarities between the two nations—and crucial dissimilarities from most nations in the world. Both Israel and America are nations by intention and by ideas. Both Israel and America are covenantal-constitutional peoples, based on freely chosen consent, sealed with a morally binding commitment, and issuing in collective solidarity with a reciprocal responsibility of all for all others. (The major difference is that Israel's covenant was directly with God as a partner, and America's covenant was only between fellow Americans, though for most citizens at the time of the revolution and many today, it was still understood that the American Constitution was "under God.") Thus, importantly, both Israel and America depend on the promise-keeping of their people to maintain their identity and continuity and to hand on their story from generation to generation, through celebration, commemoration, and education.

In sum, for both Israel and America, there is an unbreakable link between history and the heart. Moses famously set out the choice before Israel as they entered their own land. "See, I have set before you today life and prosperity, and death and adversity. . . . I have set before you life and death, the blessing and the curse. So choose life in order that you may live, you and your descendants" (Deuteronomy 30:15, 19). But tellingly,

Moses added an arresting warning that Americans must never forget: "*If your heart turns away . . .*" (Deuteronomy 30:17).

The choice was theirs. The freedom for which God had freed them from Pharaoh's slavery was real. They were now truly free, and they were responsible too, so there would be consequences. And both their freedom and its potential self-destruction would stem from the heart. When the fire of freedom is lit in the hearts of free people, it will spread through their private lives and out into their public lives and across the land. Freedom requires that the torch of freedom burns brightly in every sphere of life and at every stage of life. But if freedom is seduced and distorted in the heart, it will sooner or later die in history. Both freedom and the temptation and destruction of freedom begin in the heart.

"We the people" of America now face a similar choice. In free societies renewal is always necessary and always possible. Will some future US president do what Lincoln did in the Civil War and proclaim a National Day of Prayer and Fasting and even go on to lead America in a National Day of Atonement? Will the president preside over a ceremony of national renewal and recommitment to the covenantal-constitution? Will there be a nationwide renewal of the ceremonies of individual commitment to the covenantal-constitution, such as the Pledge of Allegiance? American minds must be involved, in that Americans have forgotten God, forgotten history, and forgotten the distinctiveness of their own freedom, but the problem lies deeper than the mind alone. American hearts have turned away from faith in God and from their great experiment, and Americans are making their choice without realizing it. Is freedom the license to do what you like or the responsibility to do what you should? Does freedom require character, truth, and a way of life, or is it best advanced by imaginations liberated from the past and from principle, imaginations that dare to break down all moral and physical boundaries, even the realities of our human bodies? The grand overarching choice before America is the choice between the ordering of 1776 and the ordering of 1789, between Sinai and Paris and thus between freedom and serfdom, between mercy and ruthlessness, between renewal and decline, and between the vine and fig tree and the hammer and sickle.

I, for one, grew up in revolutionary China and lived under Chairman Mao's version of the hammer and the sickle, so I have no hesitation in voting for the rich, personal, and local freedom of the vine and fig tree. I have also visited and observed the fate of many nations conquered or ruled by communism and the radical left, so the lesson in my mind is written in letters of fire: *the revolution of the radical left never works, and the oppression of the left never ends.* Then too I have read and listened to the utopian fantasies of borderless worlds, New World Orders, and World Republics from H. G. Wells to John Lennon, George Soros, and Klaus Schwab. Wake up, America. Your brief decades of conceited superpower daydreaming after the collapse of the Soviet Union are over. Your power is not unrivaled. You have enemies within and enemies without that are just as deadly as the Nazis and the Soviets, and their target is your freedom and the future for your children.

Your ideals as a republic and as a democracy are quite different, but you must remember what each of them requires.

Remember your history. Turn back to its best, remedy its worst, and go forward to pursue the unappeased dreams of ideals that are yet to be realized. Understand freedom, choose what freedom requires, celebrate and cherish freedom, sustain freedom, and hand on freedom so that generations of Americans to come may live under their own vine and fig tree, and enjoy the good society that is the gift of God and the fruit of well-ordered freedom.

History is putting America on notice in this generation. After the great civilizational crises of history are over, such as the decline and fall of empires and nations, there are always two questions raised: *What happened? And why didn't someone do something when the catastrophe could have been stopped?* Those questions need to be asked now, ahead of time. There is still time, though rapidly diminishing time, for Americans to raise those questions now and to think and act on the answers before it is too late.

Americans, the window of your opportunity is brief. The present moment is a moment for the ages and a moment that must not be missed. You stand before the bar of history, and history's ultimatum is before you. Do you wish to continue free, and are you prepared to do what freedom itself requires of you? The time for your choice about freedom, freedom's requirements, and your future is now. Choose wisely, and you and those who come after you may live long and well. Choose wrongly, and your decline is sure and self-chosen. Drift on and make no choice, if you like, but remember that no choice is a choice too and a bad choice. Freedom and freedom's responsibility mean that both the choice and the consequences are yours.

America, the present moment is your zero hour. The way to go forward best is to go back first. The time for your decisive choice is now. For God's sake, for history's sake, and for your children's sake, choose life and choose freedom. And choose with no further delay. Your zero hour is upon you.

INDEX

Abel, 142
Abraham, 14, 81, 82
Adam, 81, 95
Adams, John, 188
Alaric, 177
Allen, Woody, 41
Antoinette, Marie, 100
Aristotle, 107-8, 174
Bach, Johann Sebastian, 23
Bacon, Francis, 23
Belshazzar (King), 165
Berlin, Isaiah, 70
Bezos, Jeff, 54
Biden, Joe, 38, 49, 149, 160
Bloom, Claire, 41
Bloomberg, Michael, 54
Bolt, Robert, 78
Bolt, Usain, 146
Bonaparte, Napoleon, 121
Bryce, James, 30, 175
Bunyan, John, 137, 139
Burckhardt, Jacob, 25
Burke, Edmund, 125
Bush, George W., 54
Cain, 81, 96, 142
Charles, Prince of Wales, 172
Chesterton, G. K., 140
Churchill, Winston, 160
Cicero, 156
Clinton, Hillary, 54
Crow, Jim, 143
Crusoe, Robinson, 85, 86
Dante, 22, 123
David, Jacques-Louis, 121
Dawkins, Richard, 91
Defoe, Daniel, 86
Democritus, 156
Diderot, Denis, 132
Donne, John, 83
Dorsey, Thomas, 16
Dostoevsky, Fyodor, 25, 121
Douglass, Frederick, 84
Dowager (Empress), 109
Dubos, René, 47

Durkheim, Émile, 175
Eban, Abba, 35
Eichmann, Adolf, 142
Einstein, Albert, 61
Elazar, Daniel, 110
Ellul, Jacques, 49
Engels, Friedrich, 181
Eve, 95
Farrow, Mia, 41
Floyd, George, 44, 128
Foucault, Michel, 181
Franklin, Benjamin, 147, 148
Freud, Sigmund, 91
Fromm, Erich, 125
Gates, Bill, 51, 54
Ginsberg, Allen, 3
Glaucon, 32
Glubb, John, 174, 176
God, 4, 5, 8, 16, 22, 37, 54, 55, 56, 65, 72,
    75, 76-77, 80-81, 82, 87, 93-99, 101, 102,
    103-6, 110, 112, 117, 128, 130, 132, 137, 138,
    141, 150, 151, 155, 157, 158, 159, 185, 189
Gramsci, Antonio, 181
Hamilton, Alexander, 14
Hand, Learned, 188
Harari, Yuval, 91
Harris, Sam, 91, 92
Hegel, Friedrich, 120, 121, 176
Henry VIII, 78
Heschel, Abraham Joshua, 128
Hitler, Adolph, 21, 118, 171
Hobbes, Thomas, 21, 116, 122, 130, 186
Hosea, 16
Hume, David, 117
Huxley, Aldous, 25
Ibn Khaldun, 174, 175, 182
James, Lebron, 49
Jefferson, Thomas, 113
Jesus, 36, 56, 70, 104, 156, 168, 172
Jethro, 103
Johnson, Samuel, 101
Joshua, 103
Kass, Leon, 72, 103
Kennedy, John F., 143

Kennedy, Robert, 143
Kierkegaard, Søren, 11
King, Martin Luther, Jr., 84, 117, 127, 128, 143, 154
Krutch, Joseph Wood, 92-93
Laius, 90
Le Carré, John, 50
Lenin, Vladimir, 32, 171
Lennon, John, 46, 191
Leonardo da Vinci, 19, 23
Lewis, John, 128
Lincoln, Abraham, 77, 128, 130, 140, 143, 144, 177, 190
Lot, 81
Louis XVI, 171
Machiavelli, Niccolò, 23, 117
Macron, Emmanuel, 45
Maimonides, 102
Mao Zedong, 21, 109, 124, 191
Marcuse, Herbert, 181
Marinetti, F. T., 171
Marx, Karl, 23, 91
Maslow, Abraham, 103
McLaughlin, Andrew Cunningham, 188
Micah, 15-16
Michelangelo, 19, 23, 123
Mill, John Stuart, 23
Montesquieu, 124
More, Thomas, 78
Moses, 101, 102, 103, 150, 160, 189-90
Moulton, Lord, 125
Mozart, Wolfgang Amadeus, 123
Musk, Elon, 54
Newton, Isaac, 23
Noah, 82
Nobel, Alfred, 179
Oakeshott, Michael, 122
Obama, Barack, 54
Oedipus, 90
Orwell, George, 25, 32, 33, 34
Palihapitiya, Chamath, 49
Parker, Theodore, 127
Parks, Rosa, 84
Percy, Walker, 35
Phillips, Melanie, 39
Plato, 22, 32, 108, 174
Procrustes, 152
Rawls, John, 23
Reagan, Ronald, 160, 165

Reich, Wilhelm, 41, 182
Rembrandt, 23, 123
Revere, Paul, 9
Rieff, Philip, 174, 175
Rockefeller, John D., 68
Rolling Stones, 69, 73
Roth, Philip, 41
Rousseau, Jean-Jacques, 116, 122
Russell, Bertrand, 91, 92
Sacks, Jonathan, 29, 125, 126, 139, 140-41, 184, 185-86
Sade, Marquis de, 41
Schmitt, Carl, 23, 181
Schwab, Klaus, 46, 50, 118, 172, 191
Shakespeare, William, 23, 39, 123, 168
Shelley, Percy Bysshe, 126
Sima Qian, 174, 175
Skinner, B. F., 91
Smith, Adam, 186
Socrates, 11, 22
Solomon (King), 16, 17, 62
Solzhenitsyn, Aleksandr, 33-34
Sophocles, 90
Sorokin, Pitirim, 110, 135, 174, 175
Soros, George, 46, 51, 54, 118, 191
Spengler, Oswald, 174-75
Spinoza, Baruch, 90
Three Musketeers, 83, 113
Thucydides, 131
Tocqueville, Alexis de, 30
Toynbee, Arnold, 55, 118, 129-30, 173, 174, 175
Trump, Donald, 26, 38, 53, 158, 160
Tubman, Harriet, 84
Vasari, Giorgio, 19
Vico, Giambattista, 174
Voltaire, 132
Walzer, Michael, 112
Washington, Booker T., 84
Washington, George, 13, 14, 17, 18, 19, 57, 62, 65, 166
Watson, J. B., 91
Wells, H. G., 46, 118, 191
Winfrey, Oprah, 33, 170
Xi Jinping, 109, 181
Young, Andrew, 128
Zechariah, 16
Zinn, Howard, 159
Zuckerberg, Mark, 54
Zweig, Stefan, 118

ALSO BY OS GUINNESS

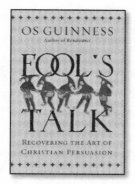

Fool's Talk
978-0-8308-4448-7

The Magna Carta of Humanity
978-0-8308-4715-0

Carpe Diem Redeemed
978-0-8308-4581-1

The Great Quest
978-1-5140-0424-1

Impossible People
978-0-8308-4465-4

Last Call for Liberty
978-0-8308-4559-0